All One
in Christ?

KT-154-283

24 JAN 1977

75 50p

All One
in Christ?

edited by
PATRICK SOOKHDEO

MARSHALL, MORGAN & SCOTT
London

MARSHALL, MORGAN & SCOTT
116 Baker Street
LONDON W1M 2BB

First published 1974
Copyright © Marshall, Morgan & Scott 1974
ISBN 0 551 05398 4

All rights reserved. No part of
this publication may be reproduced,
stored in a retrieval system, or
transmitted, in any form or by any
means, electronic, mechanical,
photocopying, recording or otherwise, without the prior permission
of the Copyright owner.

Printed in Great Britain by
Butler & Tanner Ltd, Frome and London

Contents

The Authors

PATRICK SOOKHDEO is on the staff of the Evangelical Alliance, with special responsibility for people from overseas living in Britain.

H. DERMOT MCDONALD, BA, PhD, DD, is Vice-Principal of the London Bible College

GEOFFREY GROGAN, BD, MTh, is Principal of the Bible Training Institute, Glasgow

DAVID L. E. BRONNERT, MA, PhD, BD, is Chaplain at the North London Polytechnic and on the staff of St Mary's, Islington

MORRIS STUART, DipTh, is a West Indian evangelist working in Britain

JOSEPH DANIELS, MD, is Director of the Mental Health and Counselling Center of the Christian Sanatorium in Wyckoff, New Jersey, USA

STEPHEN F. OLFORD, DD, DLitt, minister-at-large with Encounter Ministries in the USA, was formerly minister of Calvary Baptist Church, New York

ERNEST W. OLIVER is Secretary of the Evangelical Missionary Alliance and Executive Secretary of the Regions Beyond Missionary Union

WILLIAM K. VIEKMAN is Vice-President of International Students Inc. in the USA

DAVID W. TRUBY is a former Associate General Secretary of the Unevangelized Fields Mission

LEIGHTON FORD is an Associate Evangelist with the Billy Graham team

Foreword

It is a pleasure to write a foreword to this book which has been so largely inspired by my friend, Patrick Sookhdeo. It has been my privilege to know both Patrick and his wife, Rosemary, for some years, and I am full of admiration for the work they are doing. Their own happy home is proof enough that in Christ those from different racial and cultural backgrounds may find true oneness.

It is encouraging to know that in recent years evangelical Christians have shown an increasing concern to face up to the social implications of the Gospel and to grapple with questions which used largely to be left to those whose Christian stance could hardly be described as evangelical. The Bible has far more to say on many of these contemporary issues than we realise.

The contributors to this book are all widely respected for their work and witness. They have expressed themselves in their own way without any attempt at collusion. I trust that what they have written will at least provoke further thought and discussion which will, in turn, lead to positive action in the interests of good relations among people of different races. While we thank God that our laws in Britain are aimed to prevent discrimination on grounds of race, the real solution to the problem lies with ordinary people, whose prejudices often need to be dispelled. Pride in any form is detestable in the sight of God, and an air of racial superiority certainly does not befit those who profess the name of Christ. May this book in itself prove to be a help in promoting better relationships between men and women of different races.

GILBERT W. KIRBY

Preface

Race is one of the burning issues of our day. It is often said that Christians tend to lag behind in this field. The following chapters show, however, that Christians do have a voice in this thorny issue. That they are concerned about racism and injustice. That the Bible, which is the basis of their faith when correctly expounded, can speak to our times, and to the issues which have long plagued mankind. That Christ can, and does, break down the barriers that separate man from man and race from race. It is the conviction of the writers that racism is a sin against God, and as such needs to be repented of.

Although the chapters are written out of the situation in particular countries, the message they contain is relevant in most if not all parts of the world. For racism is world wide.

I am convinced that unless the issues raised in this book are taken seriously, then we are indeed in for troubled times. Unless we engage in a 'ministry of reconciliation', and show forth that love which filled the heart of our Saviour, then we ought not to lament the fact of a divided world and a divided church. I therefore commend this work to the Christian public hoping that through these pages they might see afresh some of the implications of belonging to a redeemed community and to gain a new vision of what it means to be *All One In Christ Jesus*.

PATRICK SOOKHDEO

Evangelical Responsibility and Racial Tension

H. DERMOT McDONALD

The conditions which give rise to racism are world-wide. Racism is one expression of a more fundamental human problem; the problem, that is, of human relationships. Wherever there is a minority and a majority there is always the potentiality for resentment and disharmony. The existence of otherness, of difference, is a constant and disturbing challenge; a gnawing reminder that not all our values and views are universally accepted and shared. This possibility of disharmony is not occasioned by colour differences only; it relates as much to the presence of Jews as a minority in Russia, of Protestants in Spain, of liberal socialists in Czechoslovakia, of Negroes in America and of immigrants in Britain. Whenever a minority imagines itself to be somehow repressed, and a majority imagines itself to be somewhat superior, this potentiality for disharmony can easily explode into actuality. When such a situation develops it needs all the wit of the statesman and the wisdom of the Church to subdue and to heal.

The basic cause of all disharmony is, of course, the reality of human sinfulness. Immediately man lost God, he lost his brother man: and by losing both God and man, he lost his dominion over the universe. 'There is no dominion without serving God', says Dietrich Bonhoeffer; and so it is. Man's native bias to evil finds expression in human pride, greed and vindictiveness. Had Bertrand Russell faced squarely this fact of human life, as did the late Professor Joad, he might have left out the word 'not' from his manifesto, 'Why I am not a Christian'. Russell tells in the second volume of his memoirs that he sought to educate his children without subjecting them to the iron hand of discipline. But with some surprise he admits to the failure of the operation as he witnesses their exhibitions of cruelty and destructiveness. He concludes that, 'to let children go free was to establish a reign of terror'. But Russell never came round to acknowledging the fact that there is a native 'something' in man which has to be taken into account as the ultimate cause of human disharmony and

I

discontent. It is the claim of the Christian gospel that it has the ultimate answer to this ultimate cause.

Yet there are immediate causes, both environmental and psychological, by which man's native evil can be stimulated, and for which there must be an immediate answer. Where, for example, society is so structured as to keep a minority apart, and to give to its members a feeling of not-belonging, then sooner or later, the root of bitterness which is engendered will sprout forth the shoots of rancour and violence. On the psychological level besides, when a majority fears that its position, its status quo, is being challenged by an awakening minority, the situation becomes fraught with danger. The natural and immediate reaction is to fence itself off and to make an effort to guard what it believes to be its rights and privileges. The minority finds itself the more frustrated and develops a sickening sense of rejection with the consequent loss of dignity. Such a condition calls for the best use of worldly good sense and the fullest use of spiritual power.

It is certainly the business of the state to deal with criminal elements in society and to make life safe for its citizens. The state cannot abrogate this essential reason for its existence. There is a call for softness in treating crime these days which makes little sense. The law cannot favour the rapist and the looter and especially at the expense of the victim. The guilty arsonist and the violent lawbreaker are responsible actors and cannot be regarded as the unfortunate victims of circumstances only; for there are many others in the same environment who do not resort to such criminal acts.

At the same time, while the state cannot tolerate criminal acts, society and the Church must each in its own way work together for the removal, wherever possible, of whatever causes such actions. If, then, it is the business of the state to enforce law, it is the duty of society to eliminate frustrations, and it is the task of the Church to bring redemption. It is at this point that the programmes of society for the helping of men and the proclamations of the Church for the healing of men come together. This does not mean at all that the former is to be equated with the latter. Liberal Christianity has too often and too easily identified the Church's purpose with the social programme, and the result has been to show itself as little more than a pale and spineless humanism. Evangelical Christianity, on the other hand, has too often and too easily divorced itself from social concern and shut its eyes to the raw facts of social frustrations which breed crime, and has tended to

2

justify its position by contending that such issues lie beyond and outside its purpose. Thus, if liberal Christianity has lengthened its cords by disregarding the strength of its stakes, evangelical Christianity has truly enough strengthened its stakes, but failed to lengthen its cords.

Now it is only a Christianity whose stakes are secure in the truths of the gospel which can afford to lengthen its cords. Too many church programmes have come to grief because they have not been well founded. Efforts to cast the tent over whole communities have resulted in collapse because the central theological convictions were too weak to meet the pressure. But thoughtful evangelical Christianity need not hesitate and indeed dare not do so if it takes seriously the essential biblical truths on which it stands.

In the matter of race relationships, evangelical Christianity has dragged its feet, instead of being in the lead. It should act because of the great biblical truths by which it is undergirded; the biblical doctrines of creation, providence and grace. The essence of the doctrine of creation is that this is God's world; none of us has therefore a priority claim on it. What have we more than others that we have not received? Human beings, too, made in the image of God, are made for each other. It is virtual blasphemy to sing about the red and yellow, the black and white, being 'precious in God's sight' and then despise those who differ from us in colour. The biblical declaration is that God has made of one (blood) all nations that are on the earth; what then is the presence of a minority in the midst of a people, but the God-given opportunity for that people to rise to moral heights, and to test its basic convictions amid the hard realities which such circumstances occasion? Sometimes the existence of a minority, not understood, reacts in judgment upon a nation which fails to meet aright the consequent moral challenge. The whole drift of Christ's outreach was towards the social and racial outcast while his polemic was directed for the most part towards the religious world. To regard, and to treat another, as a lesser breed without the law, is to undercut the whole biblical doctrine of redemption. For if by one (blood) all are made, is it not also by one blood that all are redeemed? In the teaching of Jesus the neighbour was one of a Samaritan minority; and he bid those who would be followers of his way to have a concern for the outsider on the roadside. Evangelical Christianity is challenged today to re-examine the strength of its stakes so that it may lengthen its cords.

3

Only by removing obstacles on the way can the Church prepare in the ghettoes a highway for our God. To regard the situation as hopeless is to court disaster and disappointment. Every predicament is but a challenge to new experiment. The Church must take risks for God with men and money. Some things men of evangelical faith must do immediately. Preachers must state, and state again, the great biblical principles which underlie its gospel and make them relevant to the issue of racism. No less must the prophetic concern for one's fellow-man against exploitation, greed and fear, be brought home to all to whom the Bible is a divine word. The message of the Epistle of James must not be suppressed for fear of offending those on whom some Christian work is thought to depend. It has a message for those who pile up wealth and fail to pay right wages and who fatten themselves like cattle.

There are practical things to be done as well, things which can only be well done by those whose stakes are secure. Young and resourceful evangelical Christians are needed, who will take seriously the challenge of the ghetto to serve as teachers and social workers. Evangelical Christians must learn to see all men simply as men, as their fundamental faith affirms.

A segregated society and a racist Church cannot survive; the former will commit suicide by internal strife; and the latter, sooner or later, will have its candle-stick removed by revealing itself a pathetic contradiction of the essence of the gospel of Christ. The Church was born in a non-racial atmosphere, drawn 'from every nation under heaven' (Acts 2:5 RSV). A racist Church is the heir of that pharisaical sectionalism against which the apostle Paul fought and in so doing laid down the principle which makes all distinctions void—'There is no such thing as Jew and Greek, slave and freeman, male and female; for you are all one person in Christ Jesus' (Gal. 3:28 NEB).

The Biblical Doctrine of Race

GEOFFREY GROGAN

The title of this chapter indicates the limited but very important area with which it is concerned. Here we are at the farthest remove from considerations of expediency. Here we address ourselves to that written authority which, as evangelical Christians, we recognise in all matters of faith and practice. And there is no doubt that the question before us is one of faith which has important repercussions in the realm of practice.

Is there such a thing as the Biblical doctrine of race? If there is, then it will be part of the Biblical doctrine of man. The latter is much wider in its scope than has often been recognised. Most treatments of it tend to concentrate on the adult individual. Its teaching about the child and about man in society are neglected, with the single exception of the doctrine of Original Sin, for it is impossible to discuss this without dealing with the social nature of man.

We will examine Scripture to see if it has a doctrine of race at all and if so what its teaching is on this subject.

I. THE OLD TESTAMENT
(a) *The creation of man*
Genesis chapters 1 and 2 reveal the unity of mankind in creation. In the sense in which the term 'race' is being employed in this book, man was obviously a non-racial being at this stage. Unlike the rest of creation, he was made in or as the image of God. The command of Genesis 1:28 implies that it was God's intention for humanity to occupy and take charge of the whole earth. Man was given authority and yet was himself under divine authority. Genesis chapter 2 shows us that man is 'from the earth, a man of dust' (1 Cor. 15:47 RSV; cf. Gen. 2:7). So, like the beasts, he has a humble origin, but unlike them (we may be warranted in assuming) he has the divine breath in him (Gen. 2:7). The marriage of Adam and Eve was grounded in their physical unity (Gen. 2:18–25), and Eve was in fact the mother of the whole

human race (Gen. 3:20). So in the creation of these two the human race was brought into being and later generations therefore emerge by the processes of natural generation. Scripture knows of only one exception to this—our Lord Jesus Christ in his virgin birth (Matt. 1:18–25; Luke 1:26–38).

Genesis 5:1–3 repeats some of the language of Genesis 1:26f and then speaks of Adam becoming the father of a son in his own likeness. This studied repetition of the language of likeness has sometimes been thought to suggest the transmission of the image of God (affected as it now was by sin) from Adam to his posterity. It could be significant that these verses occur at the beginning of the first major genealogy in Scripture (only the brief genealogy of Genesis 4:17ff precedes it). That man is still in some sense the image of God is confirmed in any case by passages like Genesis 9:6; 1 Corinthians 11:7; James 3:9 (cf. Matt. 22:20f). The exact nature of the divine image has been an important subject of discussion among theologians. For our purposes, however, the most important facts are its universality, and the fact that it shows man to have some special relationship to God. Genesis chapter 1 would seem to suggest that it is this which distinguishes man from the beasts and the rest of creation. 'Man is defined according to the divine summons of Genesis 1:26 as "the image of God", a term which denies any fundamental quality to the phenomenal difference between man and man. Man everywhere is *essentially* the same. Every distinction between man and man is secondary to the fundamental standing of every man as the image of God' (D. A. Clines, 'The Image of God in Man', *Tyndale Bulletin*, 1968, p. 94).

(b) *Before and after the Flood*

Genesis 6:1–8 is a passage which has puzzled commentators. There are at least four interpretations of note. An old Jewish view is that the sons of God were aristocrats and the daughters of men women of humble origin. Some take the sons of God to be the godly line of Seth which at this point began to intermarry with the ungodly line of Cain. A third view is that 'sons of God' should be translated rather 'sons of the gods' and that the passage refers to pagan kings who indulged in polygamy. Others take the sons of God to be fallen angels (perhaps acting through demoniac humans) who married human women. It is doubtful if any of these interpretations may properly be described as 'racial' in the sense in which the term is being used in this book. The purpose of the Flood was to remove all human life from the earth, except Noah and his family

(Gen. 6:7f). The stock that was produced as a result of these unions is referred to as if it were a thing of the past when Genesis was written (v. 4). The exact meaning of the term *Nephilim* is unknown but it should be noted that the reference to them in Numbers 13:33 does not necessarily imply that they still existed, for it occurs in the report of the ten spies, who were concerned to impress upon their hearers how fearsome the inhabitants of the land of Canaan were.

After the Flood the command is again given to multiply and fill the earth (Gen. 9:1, 7). The Noachian ordinances contain a very significant expression: 'of every man's brother I will require the life of man' (Gen. 9:5 RSV). Here alone in the Old Testament the somewhat flexible term 'brother' is used in the widest way of all, in reference to another human being as such. Moreover man's blood is sacrosanct because he is made in God's image (Gen. 9:6) and this too is true of man universally. The genealogical system of Genesis certainly seems to indicate that all who are rightly called men are descended from Noah, and so from Adam, and so are one biologically. The whole earth was peopled from the three sons of Noah (Gen. 9:18f).

Genesis 9:20–9 is of considerable importance in connection with our theme. Much has been made of Ham's immoral act and the consequent curse on Canaan. This has sometimes been used as a theological basis for regarding the Hamitic peoples as inferior to the Semitic and Japhetic groups and as being so by the judgment of God. It should be clearly noted, however, that the curse is borne by Canaan, not by Ham himself. We are not told why, but it may be that its appropriateness as a judgment on this family is due to the fact that Ham was Noah's youngest son and Canaan Ham's youngest. We cannot treat the passage as warrant for regarding the Hamites as such as doomed to subservience. Moreover the assumption so often made that the present black people are descended from Ham is itself gratuitous and quite lacking in proof. It has even been questioned whether this is in fact a divine oracle. There is no clear indication here that Noah spoke by inspiration, although of course his words are *recorded* by inspiration and they must be given to us for some purpose. Certainly the Canaanite inhabitants of Gibeon became servants of the Shemitic Israelites (Jos. 9:26f).

(c) *Babel and the dispersion of the nations* (Gen. 10–11)
Genesis 10, however we interpret it, seems to be a purely factual rather than a theological document. Four terms are used together

in verses 5, 20 and 31. These refer to geographical location, language, kinship and political division. The term translated 'family' in the RSV normally denotes a kinship group between the immediate family and the tribe. The English word 'clan' approximates fairly accurately to the sense of it. The passage draws no theological conclusions from the facts it states. In the Tower of Babel story, however, language is clearly the means of the dispersion of the people. We are not justified in inferring from the story that it is not God's will for people of different nations or races to live near each other. The Old Testament makes special provision for the sojourner (e.g. in Deut. 24:17-22).

(d) *The Song of Moses* (Deut. 32)

This great song traces the dealing of God with his people, Israel. Verses 8 and 9 declare, 'When the Most High gave to the nations their inheritance, when he separated the sons of men, he fixed the bounds of the peoples according to the number of the sons of God. For the Lord's portion is his people, Jacob his allotted heritage' (RSV). Does this refer to the scattering at Babel? This may be included, but there is a linguistic connection with Genesis 10. The word translated 'separated' here occurs in another form in Genesis 10:5, 32. The RSV translates it as 'spread' or 'spread abroad'. Can a doctrine of *apartheid* be built on this? Hardly. We would need much more evidence than this, because there is no special emphasis laid upon the notion of separation. The phrase 'sons of God' in the RSV follows the Septuagint rendering of the passage and it would perhaps link up with the teaching of Daniel that nations are presided over by different angelic beings (Dan. 10:13, 20, 21). The Hebrew however reads 'sons of Israel'. If this reading is correct, the passage would simply teach that it was the special care of God for Israel which was the chief factor in his apportionment of lands to the nations. As God divided Canaan between the tribes of Israel, so he divided the world between the nations. The most superficial knowledge of world history makes us aware of the fact that this was not a once-for-all division. Migration and movement have characterised mankind's history from the earliest times.

(e) *Old Testament Particularism*

The Old Testament is a strongly particularistic book in many ways. Israel was the people of God, upon whom he had set his love. She was called to holiness and so to a life of separation. There was to be no compromise of any kind with paganism. This is especially expounded in terms of marriage and very strong strictures against marriage with the Canaanites and other inhabitants of the land are contained in the Law (e.g. Exod. 34:11–16; Deut. 7:1–5) and in Joshua (23:11–13). There is perhaps an anticipation of this in Genesis 24. There Abraham exhorts his servant to go to Haran to find a wife for Isaac and not to take one from the people of the land. It is clear from the chapter that Abraham's relatives living in Haran were themselves worshippers of Yahweh, even though they may not have had the same depth of commitment as characterised him.

What was the reason for this marital particularism?

Wherever this is specifically given it is always religious rather than racial. It is true that this is less evident in relation to the campaign against mixed marriages carried on by Ezra and Nehemiah. In connection with this there are references to foreign women (Ezra 10:2, 14, 17f, 44; Neh. 13:23). Nevertheless, it is quite clear that the campaign had a biblical basis and that this basis was the Pentateuchal legislation, which as we have already seen, gives essentially religious reasons why there should not be intermarriage. Ezra 9:10–10:5 and Nehemiah 13:23–31 make this abundantly clear. In fact, if racially mixed marriages had been regarded as wrong per se, then we would have expected some reference to this fact in the catalogue of sexual offences in the Pentateuch. In fact there is nothing of the kind there.

(f) Old Testament Universalism

There is not only particularism but also universalism in the Old Testament. There are clear indications that God is concerned with the salvation of men and women of non-Israelite nations. These are of three kinds.

Firstly, there are elements in the legislation of the Pentateuch making provision for the spiritual needs of aliens living in the midst of the people of Israel as 'sojourners' (e.g. Exod. 20:10; 23:12; Num. 9:14; 15:14; Deut. 10:17–19, etc.). God loves the sojourner. It is true that Ammonites and Moabites were to be excluded from the religious assembly in Israel. This was, however, because of their conduct when the children of Israel were on their way to the promised land (Deut. 23:3–6; Neh. 13:1–3), and not for any truly racial reason. Moreover the prophets repeatedly denounce the sin of oppressing the non-Israelite members of the community (e.g. Jer. 7:6; Mal. 3:5).

9

Secondly, there is material in the prophets predicting the blessing of other nations through and with Israel in coming days (e.g. Isa. 2:1–4; 19:23–5). Such promises are, of course, based upon the great promise of God to Abraham that in him all the families of the earth would be blessed, or would bless themselves (Gen. 12:1–3).

Thirdly, there are plenty of instances in the Old Testament of individuals and even of groups who came into close relationship with Israel and received spiritual blessing as a result. The Kenites were a Midianite tribe or clan. To them Reuel (or Jethro), the father-in-law of Moses, belonged. Undoubtedly this group profited spiritually as well as in other ways from its association with Israel (cf. Exod. 18; Num. 10:29–32; Judg. 1:16). Names such as Rahab and Ruth come easily to mind as examples of individuals who, although born outside Israel, were brought to living faith in the God of Israel, the true and living God.

All this anticipates the teaching of the New Testament, to which we must now turn.

2. THE NEW TESTAMENT

(a) *Unity in Adam*

Romans 5:12–21 and 1 Corinthians 15:20–8, 42–50 deal with the two great heads of the race (Adam and Christ) and the consequences of their acts for those who are linked with them in a bond of solidarity. The emphasis is not so much upon oneness in creation (although this would probably be taken for granted in the case of Adam) but rather in sin and in death.

Unity in creation is clearly stated, however, in a passage in Acts which anticipates in many ways the doctrine of these two passages, that is, Paul's address on the Areopagus in Acts chapter 17. The word 'blood' (in the AV of verse 26) is probably not part of the original text. In the Greek 'one' may be either masculine or neuter. It seems likely that it is the former. In this case this sermon contains an Adam/Christ theology (cf. v. 31) and it anticipates the more developed teaching of the epistles. Paul may be attacking Athenian racial pride, for they believed that their ancestors sprang fully grown from the soil of Attica. 'No,' says Paul, 'they sprang from a common ancestor with the rest of the human race.' The second part of the verse may well be an allusion to Genesis 10 and Deuteronomy 32:8f, and will emphasise the point that God is sovereign over mankind both in terms of its history and of its geographical distribution.

(b) *Unity in Christ*

Galatians 3:28 and Colossians 3:11 refer to the unity into which men are brought in Christ. This is, of course, much deeper than that which exists in Adam. Primarily the divisions referred to in these verses are either religious (Jew, Greek) or else cultural (barbarian, Scythian). While this is true, it must also be said that prejudice tends to gather into itself other elements beside those originally in view. Because the Jew's religion was so intimately connected with his descent from Abraham his contempt for the Gentile tended to become racial as well as religious.

It is true that the religious particularism of the Old Testament was related to the distinction of Jew and Gentile. When studying the Old Testament, however, we noted that Gentiles could and did come into association with the Jews in such a way as to share Israel's covenant blessings. What these two great texts tell us is that particularism on a national basis no longer exists in Christ.

In his sermon on the day of Pentecost Peter quoted from Joel 2:28–32. Here God declares that he will pour out his Spirit upon all flesh. This great promise could be the basis for Paul's language in Galatians 3:28. The words 'neither male nor female' remind us of Joel's words, 'your sons and your daughters', 'neither slave nor free' perhaps echoes 'even upon the menservants and maidservants', while 'neither Jew nor Greek' probably interprets 'all flesh'. When we study the use of the expression 'all flesh' in the Old Testament we discover that it almost always refers to mankind as a whole. At first Peter does not seem to have seen the deeper implications of the very passage he quoted. This is by no means an isolated phenomenon in Scripture, as he himself makes clear in another passage (1 Peter 1:10–12). For this reason he was given a special revelation from God before his encounter with Cornelius and his Gentile friends (Acts chapters 10 and 11). The vision of the great sheet followed by the enquiry from Cornelius carried a clear message from God. He was not to regard any human being as 'common or unclean'. It is true that this was directed against an outlook at least partly occasioned by the particularism of the Old Testament. There is no doubt, however, that the Pharisaic outlook, which dominated contemporary Judaism at this period, had given a harshness to this particularism which is noticeably absent from the Old Testament, and Peter had been brought up under the influence of such prejudice.

Racial discrimination very often goes hand in hand with a sense of superiority on the part of one racial group. Paul's teaching in 2 Corinthians 5:16ff is highly relevant as far as this is concerned. He is saying here that the recognition of the fact that Christ died for all (v. 14) alters a man's outlook completely. He views Christ differently; he views everybody differently. He no longer looks at men from a merely human point of view (cf. 1 Samuel 16:6f). The Christian cannot look down upon any man but will view him from the vantage point of the cross.

It is a sad fact that particular racial groups are sometimes characterised by poverty and low standards of living over against others. The teaching of James 2:1–7 is relevant here. There should be no discrimination in favour of the wealthy. To act in such a way as to treat a brother Christian as inferior is quite indefensible and a sin against God.

(c) *Unity in Glory*

There are a number of passages in the Book of Revelation in which terms like 'nation' and 'language' and 'tribe' are employed together to indicate the totality of mankind (10:11; 13:7f; 14:6; 17:15ff). The book presents a glorious picture of men and women from many lands joining together in praise to the Lord God Almighty and to the Lamb in the midst of the throne (5:9f; cf. 7:9f). Here people from every tribe and tongue and people and nation constitute one kingdom and they join in the praise of him who has redeemed them. Nothing could more clearly indicate that the barriers which divide people from each other have no power to separate those who belong to each other because they belong to him. The ultimate reality is seen to be not the factors which distinguish men but the one kingdom of which they are all members and the one redemption in which they all rejoice.

Yet, impressive as such language is, it is doubtful whether it makes a significant advance in principle on that employed in Galatians 3:28 and Colossians 3:11 and this indicates the fellowship of the redeemed *here and now*. The blessing of a fellowship which bridges national and racial boundaries is the product of the reconciling work of Christ. This work lies in the past, not in the future. Such blessings flow from the Crucified Saviour *now*. Glory is simply the perfect realisation of what is already in being through the gracious activity of God in Christ. The Church is only true to its divinely appointed destiny when it remembers its international, inter-social, inter-racial character.

This does not mean, of course, that there should be a dull and monotonous uniformity about humanity, and that our styles of life should be identical. The same book tells us that the distinctive glories of the nations are to be brought into the new Jerusalem (21:24–6). Those who have known something of international fellowship are often made vividly aware of the fact that differences of cultural background may mean spiritual enrichment. The terms 'Western Christ' and 'Eastern Christ' are not altogether happy ones, and yet, because he is not just the Son of Abraham but the Son of Man, people with differing backgrounds may help each other to see aspects of his Person which others may not have glimpsed. It is only 'with all the saints' that we 'may have power to comprehend . . . what is the breadth and length and height and depth, and . . . know the love of Christ which surpasses knowledge' (Eph. 3:18, 19 RSV).

3. CONCLUSION

As we opened this chapter we asked whether in fact there is such a thing as the Biblical doctrine of race. It could perhaps be argued that our studies have yielded no evidence that there is. The question of race, abstracted from other issues, is never tackled at all in Scripture. There is no emphasis upon purely racial distinctions. Many of the prophecies of the Old Testament focus attention upon particular nations, of course, but a national and a racial interest are not identical.

What is of great importance is the fact that we have discovered nothing that could act as a support for racism of any kind. Just the opposite, in fact. The fundamental unity of humanity is explicitly taught in both the Old and the New Testaments, and is taken for granted throughout the Bible. All are created by God; all belong to each other through Adam. Harnack and other liberal writers employed the term 'the universal brotherhood of man'. The Bible does not teach this in quite the sense intended by them, for they employed it in connection with the doctrine of the universal Fatherhood of God, and there is an important sense in which by nature we are outside God's family and need to be brought into it by grace. Nevertheless, if we are not all brothers by grace we are by nature, and at least one Old Testament passage (Gen.9) uses the language of brotherhood in this broad fashion. In the New Testament the Church is presented to us as an inter-social, international and inter-racial society, and even the Jewish particularism of the Old Testament recedes into the background.

If we take the Bible teaching seriously then we must recognise its implications in terms of equality of respect and status for men of all races. We should listen to the Biblical attack on the oppression of minorities and other similar injustices. In the Church of Christ we should act as if we really believe that Christ has broken down every barrier between man and man and made us one in himself.

A History of the Church's Attitude to Race

DAVID L. E. BRONNERT

'No community has clean hands with regard to brotherhood.'
Martin Luther King.

'As Christians, we are members of a body that can know no racial barriers.' *Trevor Huddleston.*

Any sketch of the history of the Church that makes any claims to truthfulness has to include not only great achievements, but terrible failures, and much mediocrity. Some Christians have been in the forefront of concern for racial justice and harmony—a long list could be given of those who in widely different circumstances and periods of history, have given time, energy, money and suffering because of that concern. Regrettably, others have been great opponents invoking the name of Christ and quoting the Scriptures to justify a totally opposite attitude. Still others have simply reflected the opinions and practices of the community or group to which they belong; in this respect children of the world rather than children of God.

No Christian group can claim to have escaped from its share in reflecting and approving the sins against humanity and justice committed in the history of the world; and this is especially so in the realm of race relations. No denomination has a more sustained record of concern and action for racial justice than the Society of Friends—an enviable record—yet leading Quakers like George Fox and William Penn approved of slavery, the Quaker-dominated government of Pennsylvania enacted a harsh slave-code, and much Quaker wealth was built on the proceeds of the slave-trade. On the other hand, it is possible to overlook what has been achieved and write off the whole Christian endeavour as 'God's lost cause'.

There have been three recurring attitudes in the relationship of white Christians to the members of another race; oppressive, paternalistic and egalitarian. One or other of the attitudes may be more typical of one period of history rather than another, but usually all three have been present. The oppressive attitude is reflected in the long history of slavery, but is not confined to that, and is quite evident in the world today. The paternalistic attitude is typical of the colonial era; it involved a genuine idealism and concern for others without a proper respect for the independent adult will of others: 'we are here to do you good whether you like it or not'. Although the egalitarian is typical of the best of modern attitudes, it is not absent in some Christians even in the worst of earlier periods; history by no means records a uniform progress in attitudes, there has been regression as well as progress and exceptions for good or ill to prevailing trends.

So significant has slavery been in moulding modern attitudes that in considering the early history of the Church, it is essential to make some comment on it, in spite of the fact that it was not racial in its basis but economic. In the first three centuries, slavery was an important factor in society; Christians were more at the receiving end of the system than in the more modern varieties in that a large number were slaves and few of them were slave-owners (it is significant that St. Paul usually writes about the question from the viewpoint of the slave). There was a genuine egalitarianism in the Church.

> 'The Church treasury would be used to finance the manumission of slaves in bad households as also of those who became slaves by being taken prisoners of war.... In the Church masters and slaves were brethren. Several emancipated slaves rose to be bishops, notably Callistus of Rome in the third century.... Whereas under Roman law slaves could not contract a legal marriage, the Church regarded marriages between slaves and free as indissoluble.'[1]

This traditional approach had to be interpreted away in the sixteenth century to make room for very different treatment of black slaves. With the conversion of Constantine, various measures were gradually introduced that improved the lot of slaves (the measures introduced by Justinian in the sixth century are noteworthy). Eventually it ceased to have much importance, being replaced by serfdom.

In the fifteenth century slavery reappeared, Turks made slaves of Christians with the fall of Constantinople, and soon after, the Spanish, Portuguese and British introduced slavery into America.

It has been said of the Pilgrim Fathers, unfairly but with more than a grain of truth: first they fell on their knees then on the aborigines. It is unfair in that it neglects the attempts to live at peace by many, and the missionary endeavours of a number, notably John Eliot. Yet the grain of truth is that the Christians who went to America, on the whole viewed the Indians much more in the spirit of Joshua and the Israelites entering Canaan than in the spirit of Paul's missionary work among the Gentiles. The whites, like the Israelites, were leaving persecution behind; they looked on themselves as God's people entering the promised land; the Indians were the heathen to be controlled if necessary like the Canaanites. The prevailing mood among many puritans can be seen in the propositions that were passed in the New England assembly of 1640 at a discussion of 'the Indian question': The earth is the Lord's and the fullness thereof; The Lord may give the earth or any part of it to his chosen people; We are his chosen people. John Eliot is representative of many other missionaries in history whose concern for people of another race earned them obloquy from their own. Through his missionary work, he knew and respected many Indians in an intimate way, and spoke out against their enslavement: 'The design of Christ in these last days is not to extirpate nations but to gospelise them; to sell souls for money seemeth to me a dangerous enterprise.'

In America with the passage of time, Indian slaves were replaced in the scale of importance by African. The status of Indians was more open to ambiguity than that of the Africans. The Indian was assumed to be free unless it was proved otherwise, whereas the onus was on the African to prove his freedom. The initial common attitude among Christians was that the black slaves were prisoners of war, and as heathen might be legitimately enslaved; indeed slavery conferred a benefit on them as it enabled them to become Christians! With the profession of Christianity by slaves, the earlier justification ceased to be credible and the defence of slavery became overtly racist. The Bible was pressed into service; the African was a descendant of Ham and was doomed to perpetual slavery as a 'hewer of wood and drawer of water' because of the divine anger lowering over him. The traditional attitude had been that a Christian could not be enslaved by a fellow-Christian, so in early days it was thought that baptism might prove a threat to slavery. No doubt partly out of a concern for the religious welfare of slaves (slave-owners were reluctant to allow Christian instruction because it threatened their property), but undoubtedly also from the less worthy motives of self-interest and profit, it became generally accepted that conversion affected a slave's relationship to God, but not his status in society; 'spiritual' freedom did not have any implications of a material kind in this world.

Christians were involved not only in owning slaves, but in carrying out the slave-trade, and profiting from it. The great majority of those involved in the traffic in human beings were only nominal Christians, but there were those who had a real experience of God. John Newton was involved in the slave-trade after his conversion as well as before it, and he records his meeting with one or two Christians among the slavers. It was not simply that John Newton continued in his previous occupation, but he became a mate and then a captain of a slave-trader. 'During the time I was engaged in the slave-trade, I never had the least scruple as to its lawfulness. I was on the whole satisfied with it as the appointment Providence had marked out for me.' He records that no friend or acquaintance ever raised the question of the rightness of the institution of slavery—that was in the 1750s.

At this time a common attitude among evangelical Christians was that of George Whitfield; he condemned the ill-treatment of slaves by their owners in the strongest language, but accepted the institution as lawful, and he himself owned slaves. The barbarities that were inseparable from the institution come out very clearly in John Newton's journal. As captain, he sought to restrain the misuse of the women slaves by the sailors, and to treat the slaves with humanity: 'I can sincerely say that I have endeavoured to do my duty by them, without oppression, ill-language or any kind of abuse as remembering that I also have a Master in Heaven and there is no respecter of persons with him.' Humane and Christian he sought to be, and there was no conscious hypocrisy, yet he was shipping human beings, including a large number of children, as cargo; and in order to prevent a slave rebellion on ship he 'put the boys in irons and slightly in the thumbscrews to urge them to a full confession'. Custom and self-interest blinded him to what he was doing.

The latter half of the eighteenth century was the peak period for the transporting of slaves; more than half the total were carried in British ships. A country that claimed to be Christian was building its wealth and trade on slavery. An increasing volume of protest developed, as the evils that were woven into the institution became more widely known. A significant voice was that of John Wesley: 'I read a book published by an honest Quaker, on that execrable sum of all villainies, commonly called the Slave

Trade. I read of nothing like it in the heathen world, whether ancient or modern: and it infinitely exceeds, in every instance of barbarity, whatever Christian slaves suffer in Mahometan countries.' The passion and fervour of the revival moved against slavery and all that it stood for; though significant evangelical figures were opposed to the abolition—for instance Lord Dartmouth, the President of the Board of Trade. In 1788, John Newton then Rector of St. Mary Woolnoth in the city of London published his *Thoughts upon the African Slave Trade*. His own previous experience and heavy involvement in slavery made it an especially powerful critique; in many ways it is a model Christian confession of sin, written without seeking to excuse his failures, and without attempting to exaggerate the evils. His motives are clear: 'I am bound in conscience to take shame to myself by a public confession, which, however sincere, comes too late to prevent or repair the misery and mischief to which I have, formerly, been accessory.' The Christian convictions that lie behind this public confession are evident from the opening quotations, ' "All things whatsoever ye would that men should do to you, do ye even so to them; for this is the law and the prophets." "Homo sum." ' He now saw slavery in its true colours, 'a commerce so iniquitous, so cruel, so oppressive, so destructive'. The story is well known of how William Wilberforce sought an interview with him, and as a result committed himself to Christ and devoted his life to the abolition of slavery. It is salutary to remember that not all evangelicals were in the abolitionist camp; Dabney in his *Evangelical Theology* (reprinted by the Banner of Truth in 1969) gave a vitriolic defence of slavery with many aggressively anti-black comments. Even so, the abolition of slavery did represent a triumph of Christian convictions over custom, self-interest, prejudice—and even over the Christians!

The nineteenth century was a period of great expansion in missionary endeavour; the dominant attitude of white to black was unquestionably paternalistic. A not-untypical missionary report in 1822 shows the white Christians introducing the British system of education, teaching the Polynesians to make and wear 'neat hats and bonnets in the European form', and deploring 'the indolent habit' of the islanders in taking a siesta. The unwritten assumption was that the European custom and culture was the best, and was an automatic part of progress towards civilisation. The other half of paternalism was also there, a genuine concern for the people and a longing to share the gospel. The Polynesian

Christians were regarded as 'brethren', and although in practice it was interpreted as meaning less than equal, the idea contained the seeds of equal dignity and worth. There were exceptional Christians like Hudson Taylor who had a real appreciation of the value of non-European culture, and attempted in a literal way to disengage the gospel from its European dress. In the early days of the China Inland Mission, racial inter-marriage was accepted as perfectly in order for the Christian; though a ban was introduced at a later date and only rescinded recently. Christian missionaries not infrequently incurred the wrath of their fellow-countrymen by siding with their fellow-Christians against injustice; a report from South Africa in 1852 comments:

'the conduct of the Colonists has been calculated to produce in the minds of the coloured people, distrust, estrangement, and enmity. They had manifested very strongly the prejudices which many English showed towards the coloured people. The malignity and violence of the Colonists have not been restricted to the native tribes, but several of our missionaries have been assailed with vulgar clamour and brute force.'

With the ending of slavery in America, and the progress of the gospel in South Africa, segregated churches developed. As long as the black population was directly controlled by the white, the issue did not arise, but with black emancipation the white-controlled churches in America discriminated. Seats were set apart marked 'BM' (black member), and very soon separate congregations developed. In South Africa, the Dutch Reformed Church accepted that it was biblical for black and white to worship together, but conceded the possibility of segregated worship in view of the prejudices of some white Christians. Its synod in 1857 declared:

'The Synod considers it desirable and scriptural that our members from the Heathen be received and absorbed into our existing congregations wherever possible; but where this measure as a result of the weakness of some, impedes the furtherance of the cause of Christ among the Heathen, the congregation from the Heathen, already founded or still to be founded, shall enjoy its Christian privileges in a separate building or institution.'

The consequences in both countries were to be long-standing both in church life and in society; concessions to white prejudice far from removing the strength of feeling behind it, gave it legitimacy. So much so, that evangelical theology became intertwined with white supremacy; as recently as 1960 Wheaton College in America refused to graduate a black student for marrying a white, and in 1966 a congregation expelled its ministers for proposing that black Christians be allowed to join in worship. Of course in America in the 1960s, the theory of segregation has been rejected but the realities and the attitudes often remain much the same.

Whatever might be the attitude of individual missionaries, the dominant attitude of white Christians in the nineteenth and first part of the twentieth century was paternalistic. Alfred Noyes expressed British Christian feeling, when he wrote:

> *Hasten the Kingdom, England;*
> *Look up across the narrow seas,*
> *Across the great white nations to thy dark imperial throne*
> *Where now three hundred million souls attend on thine august decrees*
> *Ah, bow thine head in humbleness, the Kingdom is thine own;*
> *Not for the pride of power*
> *God gave thee this in dower;*
> *But, now the West and East have met and wept their mortal loss,*
> *Now that their tears have spoken*
> *And the long dumb spell is broken,*
> *Is it nothing that thy banner bears the red, eternal cross?*

Britain and British Christians have a divine commission to guide others for their good and eternal welfare! Along with this assumption that what was white was superior, went the conviction that blackness was undesirable. The long-standing cultural identification of black with evil (seen in such language as blackmail, blackleg, black magic as opposed to white lies, white magic, and 'white man') was accepted as part of the proper presentation of the Christian gospel; black represented sin and white righteousness.

The latter part of the twentieth century has seen considerable changes in approach; the rapid disappearance of the old-style colonial empires and the rise of black consciousness in many parts of the world made change inevitable. The attitude of Hudson Taylor that had been regarded as eccentric by many of his fellow-Christians was widely accepted as right—British culture was no part of the gospel, other cultures were not to be derided or dismissed. It was no longer assumed that white Christians had a divinely-given duty to rule, rather it was customary to talk of missionaries working under or alongside native Christians. Segregation, in theory or in practice, has been seen by the larger portion of Christians as a denial of the gospel's claim to unite all in Christ. The older attitudes remain even in the midst of egalitarianism; a revealing comment in a letter, 'Let me say, with complete integrity, that I receive coloured people of any nationality with utmost goodwill as I do all underprivileged people.'

The movement has not however been only one way; in Southern Africa the shift has been in quite a different direction. Basil Mathews writing in 1924, comments, 'The race-hatred of South Africa and Rhodesia is due to three things mainly: the loss of land, the refusal of a share in government, and the refusal by white labour of the African's right to do skilled work.' A modern commentator would not thus far wish to express himself differently, but then Basil Mathews goes on, 'By law there is no colour-bar; in practice white labour insists on the colour-bar.' Since 1948, apartheid has been accepted by the majority of the white electorate as the right policy; and the force of law has increasingly been behind separation. The result on Christians has been this:

> 'The outward values and customs of apartheid society, being phenomena which are the everyday experience of the members tend often to have a stronger impact than the spoken Word of God. . . . Apartheid tends to deaden any sense of the community of mankind and that basic fellowship of all Christians in Christ, which is irrespective of colour, race and sex. This in turn, makes them unaware of their need to serve each other as brothers. Apartheid fosters a false sense of white supremacy . . . It encourages the practice of paternalism, discrimination and injustice, breeds intolerance, prejudice and violence, and encourages fear and dislike of the unlike.'[2]

Many church leaders have expressed opposition, and a good number have suffered in various ways as a result; evangelicals have been much more quiescent sometimes to the extent of explicit support for apartheid. In America as well as in South Africa, rank-and-file white Christians have been less inclined to act in accordance with multi-racial principles. The Dutch Reformed Churches in South Africa have continued to support apartheid, though individuals have dissented; 'it is in complete accord with the Scriptures that peoples should protect themselves for the sake of their God-given calling . . . Mixing is a sin if it threatens Christian or historically valuable culture . . . Races and nations mixing as a principle and rule in church circles must be rejected.'[3]

A similar variation in attitudes can be seen in Britain, even though the legal position is totally different; a very strong lead in an egalitarian direction has been given by church leaders, this time including well-known evangelicals such as David Sheppard, with lay attitudes much more commonly reflecting the prejudices of the white population. There has been without doubt a general shift away from exploitation, and paternalism, among Christians as a whole; but especially among black Christians. The rise of black consciousness has meant, especially among younger and better-educated blacks, the refusal to accept an inferior status, and a rejection of paternalism even when disguised as liberalism.

'The problem is not blackness but white racism . . . The reaction of the Christian black is one of forgiveness through love for the past, and a search for justice through radical application of the Christian faith—showing in attitudes as well as actions that God is as determined as we are to effect the necessary social transformation' (Morris Stuart).

1. Henry Chadwick, *The Early Church* (Pelican, 1967), p. 60
2. Ed. Peter Randall, *Apartheid and the Church* (Spro-cas, Johannesburg, 1972), p. 17
3. Gordon Harris quotes 'Gereformeerde Kerk in Suid Afrika', in *Race and Evangelical Christians in South Africa* (ERRG private circulation), p. 6

The Contemporary Church and Race

MORRIS STUART

'We recognise the failure of many of us in the recent past to speak with sufficient clarity and force upon the biblical unity of the human race. . . . We reject the notion that men are unequal because of distinction of race or colour. In the name of the Scriptures and of Jesus Christ we condemn racism wherever it appears. . . . We extend our hands to each other in love, and those same hands reach out to men everywhere with the prayer that the Prince of Peace may soon unite our sorely divided world' (Extract from a statement from the Berlin Congress on Evangelism 1966).

'When men of privilege abuse their power and refuse justice, sooner or later violent upheaval is bound to come. If we do not seek to heal the gaping rubber-raw wounds of racial strife, then we shall deserve "the fire next time" (Leighton Ford—Minneapolis Congress on Evangelism 1969).

The current attitude of the church towards race relations is one of growing idealism and critical self-examination in an atmosphere of widespread conservatism and indifference. It is customary nowadays for Christian assemblies and congresses to discuss and issue statements on Christian social involvement. And in recent years evangelicals have become increasingly recommitted and vocal concerning this aspect of Christian witness. There is a growing reaction to that attitude which, in the twentieth century, has isolated evangelism from social action, to the almost total exclusion of the latter.

'Our social action must neither replace our evangelism, nor must it simply be regarded as a springboard for our evangelism. It is not social action *or* evangelism, nor is it social action *for* evangelism, we must engage in social action *and* evangelism, because . . . we have two commissions to fulfil, the commission of compassion, and the commission of evangelism (Mt. 25:34-6, and 28:20)' (Morecambe Conference on Evangelism 1972).

However, even in this atmosphere of rediscovering the prophetic[1] role of the Church concerning man in society, there are many who counsel, 'preach the gospel, and don't dabble in politics'. Others, because they have assumed—mistakenly—that an evangelical conservatism of necessity demands as a consequence a social conservatism, have sought to express a Christianity which is reflective of, rather than reformative in its effect upon the society in which they find themselves. This unbiblical concept of Christianity in the context of society, has frequently led to a blind-spot in Christians in their attitude to race relations.

Coloured immigration to Britain, which began in the early 1950s, brought the challenge of race relations forcibly to the British Church. In his book *World Aflame*, Dr. Billy Graham said, 'Great Britain has always prided itself on being free of racial prejudice. However, when thousands of coloured peoples moved into the British Isles, the Britons found that they had plenty of prejudice.' And—with some notable exceptions—Christians, and especially conservative evangelicals, cannot lay any claim to have behaved significantly differently from their compatriots in their reactions to the newcomers.

One fact of the Church's current experience of 'race', is the existence of two churches, one black, the other white. Attitudes toward the black church in Britain tend to be schizophrenic, ranging from outright condemnation to disguised paternalism. On the one hand these groups are labelled racists and separatists, on the other it is said patronisingly, 'but, the coloured folk would not feel at home in our services, they like to worship in their own way'.

But to charge the black churches with racism and separatism is to misunderstand why they came into being, and why they continue to grow. All the main groups were established denominations in the West Indies; especially is this so of the New Testament Church of God, whose roots go back to the Church of God, Cleveland Tennesee. Because of the 'carry-over' factor, the establishment of these churches in Britain was inevitable. To this must also be added the rejection in the form of non-acceptance rather than overt hostility by the 'host' church of many coloured believers. This rejection may well have produced a reaction, but the apparent racial character of the church has its explanation in rejection rather than separation.[2] Clifford Hill has shown,[3] and many others have observed, that although these groups were *established* in the 1950s, they did not begin to attract large numbers of immigrants until 1964.

Revival and intensified evangelism may well have played a part in this sudden increase in numbers, but it is important to note that it was in 1964 that 'race' became explicitly an election issue, and coloured churchgoers perceived in the attitudes of white Christians the same attitudes which were evident in some politicians. The mainstream denominations lost coloured members and adherents, and the black church gained in almost proportionate numbers.[4]

The attitude which says, 'but they like to worship in their own way' also springs from a misunderstanding. While it is true that many West Indian believers were discouraged by the coldness and formality of English church services, worship forms were not the main reason for the formation of black churches. The emotional excesses which are sometimes seen in black churches can be duplicated with equal precision in some white Pentecostal congregations.[5] A fact which is not widely known, is that whereas in Britain sixty per cent of the churchgoing West Indian population attend black churches, in the West Indies over ninety per cent of the churchgoing population belong to the mainstream denominations, where hand-clapping, 'Amens', 'Hallelujahs', and 'Praise the Lords' are conspicuous by their absence. The only difference between the mainstream churches in the West Indies and their British counterparts, is that their services radiate a warmth, a sincerity and a reality which too often is almost totally absent from the worship of the indigenous British church. In any case, the West Indian population in Britain as a whole does not identify with the black church, and usually disapproves of some of its ideas.

Far from being a racist church catering for the cultural needs of West Indians, the black church is a body of evangelical believers who have been thrown together by a common church background in their country of origin and the experience of being rejected on racial grounds by the white churches. White Christians would do well to recognise the black church for what it is, and in repentance for past injuries stretch out the hand of love and fellowship for our common task of reaching our society for Christ. The black church will not disappear. One of its leaders said recently, 'We are no longer a motley band of individualists as we were in the early days, we are a mighty army, a force to be reckoned with, we are here to stay!' The black church is!

Having cleared up the misapprehensions, however, black and white Christians must realise that we belong to one Church, and

26

clearly, the scriptural and attainable ideal is not a black church or a white church, but *the* Church. This leads us on to consider integration in our churches.

The unity of believers irrespective of race is fundamental to any discussion or action concerning integration in our churches. There are two questions which have to be faced and answered. Is it scriptural—hence right? Is it practicable? The principle of unity is universally accepted, but many would say that it is neither necessary nor desirable to demonstrate this principle in practice. Because of this, stress is laid on the 'invisible' unity of the true Church.

This stress upon invisible unity is best exemplified by the South African situation, and that of the 'Bible belt' churches in the southern states of America. It is self-evident to the perceptive observer that in these contexts, commitment to invisible unity has more basis in racial prejudice than in respect for different cultures. Invisible unity is at best an admission of failure, at worst a cover up for the shameful concession which has been made to racist attitudes. To our shame it is but a euphemism for non-existent unity. This attitude is not limited to South Africa or the southern states of America. It is so important in moulding attitudes to integration, that it is essential for all Christians everywhere to look at the teaching and experience of the early Church for our guidance.

At the heart of the Christian message comes this astounding claim: 'The word became flesh and dwelt among us.' Shadow became substance, concept became reality; the love of God became a man, the holiness of God became a cross, and the power of God became a resurrection. Christianity's great claim over other religions is that it is a faith of realities, and not simply a religion of ideas. It either functions because it is real, or it ceases to function. Nowhere in the New Testament is our invisible unity spoken of as a concept, an exclusively other-worldly ideal. Nor is it there by implication. It is a mystical unity with eternal as well as temporal expressions. 'For by one Spirit we were all baptised into one body—Jews or Greeks, slaves or free . . . You are the body of Christ and individually members of it' (1 Cor. 12:13, 27 RSV). 'For Christ himself has brought us peace, by making Jews and Gentiles one people. With his own body he broke down the wall that separated them and kept them enemies . . . by means of the cross he united both races into one single body and brought them back to God' (Eph. 2:14, 16b TEV).

This mystical unity expressed itself practically and visibly in a common corporate life. Among the leaders of the church community at Antioch were two Africans, two Jews and a member of the ruling aristocracy. Discrimination at the congregational level was condemned (Jas. 2:1–7). Paul rebuked Peter in public when he saw the latter behaving in a manner which denied the truth of the gospel. Peter's action was quasi-racial in character, although the critical issue here was the circumcision (Gal. 2:11–14). The experience of the early Church was that mystical unity expressed itself in visible unity across *all* barriers, the most important of which was racial.[6] The experience of the early Church shows that integration was both right and practicable. No distinction was made between the principle of unity and its practice. Racial integration was not an optional part of the gospel. Yet modern Christians conceive it to be expedient and even necessary to develop and maintain racially distinct churches.

Authorities on church growth have suggested—very persuasively too—that racially and culturally distinct churches make for more efficient evangelism, and modern missionary strategy is increasingly being modelled on this idea. In India for example, it was observed that evangelism was carried out more 'efficiently' when done along 'caste lines'. From this and other broadly similar observations in a variety of missionary contexts, the idea was evolved that a racially distinct church would be a more efficiently evangelising church. The progression can easily be seen—low castes can best evangelise low castes, high castes their kind, Indians their kind, Africans their kind—and inevitably the position is arrived at that whites best evangelise whites, blacks best evangelise blacks; racially—and culturally—distinct churches make for more efficient evangelism, so they are the ideal to which all effort should be directed . . . QED.

This hypothesis is of crucial importance to the discussion on integration precisely because it is often used to discourage or even actively oppose it. Three criticisms have to be made. Firstly, it is vitally important to recognise that *culture is always secondary to Christ.* Jesus Christ may enhance or even confirm our culture. More often however, he stands in judgment over it. Turning to the Indian situation again; here the Church exploited something within the culture—the caste system—and observed that evangelism was successful. But to make a principle of the experience gained from this local situation, it must be shown that the framework of this local observation was morally right. The caste system could quite clearly be challenged on scriptural grounds for its moral bankruptcy. Why then, for the 'expedience' of efficient evangelism, should the truth of the gospel be denied by developing and maintaining a church which not only appears to approve an evil system, but also reflects it? Furthermore, why add to that denial by making of this local experience a principle to be applied universally?

Secondly, this idea may quite rightly be applied to the task of making the missionary church indigenous. Here, the motivation would be to evolve a Christianity which is free from the cultural and racial domination of the missionary-sending country, *and not to produce a racially or culturally distinct church*. A truly indigenous church is not a West Indian church, or an Asian church, or an African church, but *the* Church, the body of Christ in local expression. Understood in this way, national churches would not be regarded primarily as racially or culturally distinct. The *intention* of the Church's evangelism should never be to create racially distinct churches even if under certain circumstances the *effect* is to produce them. Racially orientated evangelisation produces racially orientated, even racially prejudiced, congregations!

Thirdly, there would have to be a proven scriptural precedent for this principle. The most fundamental question will have to be asked. Is it right to sacrifice the truth of the gospel—that is, the unity both mystical and material of believers for the expediency of efficient evangelism? Is the truth of the gospel not more important than the efficient winning of souls? (And here I am speaking as an incurable evangelist!)

When all the arguments for distinct churches have been considered—language, culture, and even race,—it has to be scripturally affirmed that such churches are less than ideal. It is a fact attested by the experience of committed Christians that it is not white Christians who best evangelise white non-Christians, nor black Christians who best evangelise black non-Christians, but Christians—whoever and wherever they are—who best evangelise non-Christians. It is the Spirit of God within a man who reaches the man without the Spirit of God and brings him to Christ. This is the attainable ideal. Why set aims lower than the heights which the Lord himself laid down? The church at Antioch was a multi-racial, multi-cultural, multi-class, integrated church, and a vigorous witnessing centre. Their integrated fellowship was both an attracting and challenging testimony to the society around them.

29

Clearly then, the case for developing and maintaining racially distinct churches is challengeable. And it must be recognised that efficient evangelism is not the prime task of the Church. It cannot be too strongly stressed that a racially or culturally distinct church, where the prime reason for its distinctiveness is racial or cultural, is something *less than a church*. If the reality of the scriptural truth of the unity of all believers is to be realised and expressed, integration in church life in a polyglot society is essential.

American churches have long been the battleground for racial integration. It has been cynically said that the most segregated hour in America is 11 a.m. to 12 noon on Sunday—everyone talking about unity in Christ in their separate churches. Both ethnic churches share blame. However, the white churches—and especially the Evangelical Protestant Church—have a greater responsibility for blame precisely because they have been the innovators and exponents of discrimination and prejudice within the Church. Dr. Leighton Ford, at the Minneapolis Congress on Evangelism, said, 'What kind of gospel are we preaching when a church sends missionaries to convert Africans, but suggests to the Afro-American that he go to a church with his own kind?' Churches have been split, pastors have been sacked, the aid of the civil authorities has been sought, for what? To maintain the obscene doctrine that God is white, and his chosen people are white, except those benighted blacks who are uncivilised, in need of salvation, and thank our white God, thousands of miles overseas!

Positively, however, many white churches and Christian men of both races have taken a courageous stand for the gospel, love and justice, showing to the Church and to the world the quality of faith and practice which is needed to understand and face the challenge of the racial revolution.

In Britain the reaction has been somewhat different. Many of our churches are integrated, many more are only superficially integrated. The question which must now be asked is this: is integration enough?

What does integration consist of? Martin Luther King described integration as that situation where a man is judged not by the colour of his skin, but by the content of his character. It is necessary, however, to spell out the implications of this statement. Integration does not mean having a containable minority in the Sunday morning congregation; rather it is sharing together in the worship *as well as the leadership* of the Church in its local and national expressions. A truly integrated church is not simply a church which comprises coloured as well as white members, but one in which there is coloured leadership alongside white leadership (i.e. coloured elders, deacons, church officers, and—as God will inevitably so lead—pastors and ministers). And their positions of leadership would not necessarily be achieved by means of a quota system.

It is certainly debatable whether many churches, even some 'integrated' churches, would have a coloured minister. Especially is this true in denominations without central control. On the available evidence, it would be fair to state that there are very few. There are some missionary-sending churches who would refuse to sit under the ministry of a coloured man even on an occasional basis, except of course within the context of the 'missionary' weekend.[7] By what process of reasoning is the conclusion arrived at that Europeans as missionaries could pioneer and develop missionary work overseas, but that it certainly could not enter into the head of God to send coloured men here to minister—other than to *their own folk*? The Western church must quickly accept the fact that God is already sending missionaries from Africa, Asia, the Caribbean and Latin America. If the spirit as well as the letter of integration is to be fulfilled, the Church must be seen to be integrated not only in its local expression but especially in its national bodies, its specialist evangelistic organisations and its missionary societies. Many—too many—missionary societies on both sides of the Atlantic continue to hedge over, or even absolutely refuse to consider, appointing coloured missionaries. The reasons for this policy vary from fear of inter-racial marriage among missionaries, to the fear that, for example in Africa, black missionaries would not be acceptable to Africans. All of these reasons are, however, unimportant and ill-founded, with more substance in racial prejudice than in a concern for the gospel.[8] God has handed down some stern judgments to individuals and churches who have sinned in this regard, and continued stubbornness may well bring about his anger. In the 1954 Nashville crusade Dr. Billy Graham said: 'We have become a proud race—we have been proud and thought we were better than any other race, any other people. Ladies and gentlemen, we are going to stumble into hell because of our pride.'

It is an affront to the revealed character of God to refuse any man the opportunity of serving God within the fellowship of his Church on grounds other than his spiritual character. To do this is to assault the dignity of a man who is the image of God. Racial integration is nothing less than total acceptance, and the sharing of the functions and offices of the church on the basis of complete equality. This applies even in areas where everyone is white! Integration, if it is to be meaningful, cannot co-exist with inequality. It is a farce to claim that churches are integrated while simultaneously rejecting the probability of the leadership of coloured Christians.

Integration in church life is therefore both highly desirable and essential. Where it has been achieved in a truly Christian spirit, it has proved to be eminently practicable, and far from being a liability, it has been an asset in the work of the gospel. It behoves Christians everywhere to work and pray unstintingly toward this goal.

There is yet one other area which needs to be looked at, and that concerns the fulfilment of the prophetic role of the Church in society. Proceeding from integration in Church, it is necessary to examine the Church's role in race relations in society.

No Christian is so naive as to believe that, under the present scheme of things, society will ever be free of sin and injustice. Man, affected as he is in the totality of his nature by sin, cannot by his self-effort achieve Utopia. But, man is the image of God and as such possesses the facility of moral choice. He chooses to do evil as well as good. And certainly he responds to good. Christians should give a bold lead in the realm of race relations, and so prove to be the light of the world. The modern Church—especially the Evangelical Protestant Church—constantly drags its feet, is often outdated in its approach, and is usually on the wrong side of the fence concerning the most challenging social issues. Mankind has rejected slavery as an inhuman institution, and it will reject racial discrimination too. In the struggle for this rejection, it is necessary for Christians to be the major reformers.

It is unquestionably right to affirm that an unjust society can effectively be changed only as the men and women who comprise that society are themselves radically changed. But bitter experience has shown that, although regeneration is the dynamic for social reform, it does not always lead to it, because it is considered convenient to accept Jesus as Saviour without obeying him as Lord, or submitting to him as king. Furthermore, Christians are nowhere instructed to neglect their reformative role in society either because of an exclusive emphasis on evangelism, or because their evangelism has 'failed' to win men to Christ. Christ's followers are fishers of men as well as salt of the earth. It is dishonest to paralyse Christian action with the dogma that society is incapable of any meaningful experience of racial understanding and tolerance. Clearly many non-believers possess a tolerance and an understanding which puts many Christians to shame. Despite the fall and its consequences, Christians engage in the struggle for racial justice—indeed all social justice—because of 'creation ethics', i.e. that God is maker, ruler and judge of *all* men, and our times are in his hands. Therefore Christians can challenge society to practise racial justice because society is the arena of God's activity no less than the Church is the arena of his grace.

Individual compassionate action is inadequate as a way of expressing concern. Christians tend, commendably, to major in patching up the casualties of our society, but fight shy of prophetically engaging the evil 'systems' which create these casualties. Thus the solution of the problems of race is usually seen in terms of a ministry of compassion by the Christian individual. While this is important, it must be recognised that racism is most disastrous in its effects upon people through the structures of society, the entire fabric of which is affected by it. These structures therefore should be the targets for prophetic denunciation and militant Christian action. And only corporate Christian action will have the desired effect.

Rightly or wrongly, immigration has always been at the centre of any discussion on race relations in Britain. As attitudes to immigration tend to mould attitudes to race relations—especially in non-Church circles—it would help if certain issues were clarified. Firstly, the term 'immigrant' is not a synonym for black and should never be so used. Only one in three immigrants is coloured. Secondly concerning numbers; the 1971 census showed 1·5 million people who either originated from the New Commonwealth or were descendants of people who came from there. This means a ratio of 2:100, coloured:white of the population of these islands. In any case there are currently more West Indians leaving Britain than there are work-voucher holders coming from the West Indies to settle permanently in Britain. The heart of the matter is that the numbers debate is irrelevant, with more basis in emotion than in fact.

Thirdly, the need in Britain for more labour, skilled and unskilled, is the prime reason, over and above factors in the countries of origin, for coloured immigration to Britain. They were invited or at least actively encouraged; certainly some were recruited to come to Britain. During his term of office as Minister of Health, the politician currently most associated with the immigration debate, had recruitment drives for doctors and nurses in the West Indies, Pakistan and India, so that he could build up a prestigious National Health Service. Not a word in those days about 'voluntary repatriation'. Christians should enquire into his political duplicity and opportunism before giving him their uncritical support.

Fourthly, the contribution of coloured immigrants is disproportionate to their benefits. Because as a general rule they are young, mobile and employable, they contribute more to the economy and the social services than they extract. For the forseeable future immigrants will contribute in real terms twenty per cent more to the material benefit of Britain than the population as a whole! Because their family structure and discipline is 'Victorian' the crime rate is the same as, and in some cases—Pakistanis—lower than that of the population as a whole. If coloured immigrants are treated justly, these figures will be maintained.

Immigration, its social consequences and its problems, leave the Christian no ground for unhealthy attitudes to race relations. The history of Britain with its Empire and world power status has bequeathed us the inevitable legacy of a multi-racial society. It is irrelevant to debate whether we should or should not have such a society. A multi-racial society need not be, indeed is not, a tragedy. Britain has a unique opportunity to show that a multi-racial society does work. Christians who mean business will have no time for the humbug of 'voluntary repatriation' with its patronising 'You do not belong here, nor can you, because you are black, and if given sufficient money you will go' attitude. This only stirs up hostility.

Mr. Roy Jenkins has defined integration as '. . . not a flattening out process of assimilation but equal opportunity accompanied by cultural diversity, in an atmosphere of mutual tolerance'. This should be our dream and the objective to which we should work. Or better still, Christians should by their preaching, practice and attitudes show that they are working towards that great ideal: '. . . behold, a great multitude which no man could number, from every nation, from all tribes and peoples and tongues, standing before the throne and before the Lamb, clothed in white robes, with palm branches in their hands, and crying out with a loud voice, "Salvation belongs to our God who sits upon the throne, and to the Lamb!"' (Rev. 7:9–10 RSV.)

In the racial crisis, Christians, whatever their colour, do not have the luxury of a choice. Their Lord, his gospel and his cross demand that they involve themselves at the deepest and most explosive levels. But they never engage thus on their own. By his cross and resurrection Jesus defeated and overcame all the forces of human prejudice and fear. He now lives, and indwells his people with all the authority of heaven and earth. It is this power and Presence that enters with us into the arena of the racial revolution. He *is* with us, so, GO UP.

1. The word '*prophetic*' is not used in this chapter in the predictive sense, i.e. *foretelling* the future. Rather it is everywhere used in the sense of *forthtelling*, i.e. telling forth the will and mind of God in a contemporary situation, in the tradition of the eighth-century prophets, and Jesus' Teachings in the synoptic gospels

2. Several people known personally to the writer were either asked not to come back to church services, or it was made very obvious that they were not welcome. One leading black church leader was barred from ministering in one church when the deacons discovered his colour. One London church refused a request from a leading West Indian Christian to allow West Indians to worship with them. The result, a black church was formed, which now caters for coloured as well as white people

3. Clifford Hill (Senior lecturer in Sociology of Religion N.E. London Polytechnic) 'Immigrant sect development in Britain: A case of status deprivation?'

4. Concerning the relationship between black church growth and 'felt' racial animosity, two South London ministers in an area of immigrant settlement noticed a sharp decline in the interest and attendance of coloured people to their churches immediately following Mr. Enoch Powell's 'river Tiber flowing with blood' speech in 1968. This local situation is not atypical. Also one black denomination has experienced a 1,000 per cent increase in adherents and membership since 1964

5. A New Zealand friend of the writer was once worshipping in an all white Pentecostal congregation. The worship was so noisy that she screamed—literally—for five minutes and no other worshipper took the slightest bit of notice. This is not an isolated case

6. It has been shown by the Rev. Geoffrey Grogan that Jewish religious separation tended to gather to itself elements of racial prejudice See 'unity in Christ' p. 11

7. The writer's evangelistic ministry is exclusively in 'white' churches—I have never preached or worshipped in a black church. Yet some Surrey churches refused my ministry on racial grounds. Some English minister friends of mine have told me that they know of several churches who would refuse the ministry of coloured Christians

8. A good discussion of race and missionary societies is contained in: Howard O. Jones, *Shall we overcome?* (Fleming H. Revell Co.), 1966

The Psychodynamics of Racism

JOSEPH DANIELS

Dear White Man:

Although we have known each other for centuries, we have not truly known each other. I, the black man, feel I know more about you because I had to. My will to survive forced me to learn about you. I was forced to learn your ways of doing things, forced to accept your concepts and values, and yet denied the right to share them. From my youth I have heard the phrase 'white is right', sometimes said in jest, but many times said with a sarcasm that can be detected only by the black man.

Do you really want to know me? I find I am sceptical—doubt that you do. Perhaps this in itself reveals some of my own psychopathology. Both you and I are suffering from the effects of many years of the poisoning of racial prejudice.

If I express my feelings and thoughts, can you understand them? Much of your conception of me has an illogical basis, and the more I tell you about myself, the more you may use this against me. Yes, I mistrust you, because of the way you deceive yourself, and the way you have failed to look into your heart.

If I tell you that I have hostility and anger within me, how do you interpret those emotions? Do they make me a savage who will riot and burn your property? Do you ask yourself the cause of the hostility? I ask myself this question, and offer answers that at times satisfy me and at times do not. I too have become somewhat illogical, as I attempt to handle my frustrations.

No doubt some of my hostility is the outgrowth of remembering the degrading names of my youth. Could I really have accepted the reply my mother told me to give—'Sticks and stones may break my bones, but names will never hurt me'? You taught your children to hate me, and so they hurt me. When I struck out to hurt them back, I was punished by the white teacher. Can you understand the frustration of a black child caught in this situation and not knowing how to express what he feels in words? Observe his actions; they are the only way he can express his anger.

36

Lying somewhat deeper in this substratum of hostility are the names you made me call myself. Sometimes directly, sometimes subtly, you programmed into my early years a feeling of self-dislike, even self-hatred, and deep inferiority, so that I could not accept what God made me to be. I ask you, how does one get to know who or what he is when his society distorts what he is and tries to shape his life to prove this distortion? To the extent that a society hinders a person from developing to his God-given potential, it sins not only against that person but against God. It seems to me that our society is presently paying for the many years of wrongs done to the black man.

At times I am afraid of my anger and hostility because I don't know what form it will or should take, and I don't know if I will be able to hold it in check. Like Hamlet I ask myself 'whether 'tis nobler in the mind to suffer the slings and arrows of outrageous fortune, or to take arms against a sea of troubles. . . .'

In my rational moments, I can understand that you are a product of your forefathers' teachings, and are not entirely to blame for your feelings towards me. But if you or I should pass feelings of racial hatred to our children, we stand condemned before God.

I, the black man, am beginning to see my children develop a sense of worth, and respect for their racial heritage, and this above all gives me hope for the future.

Why have you distorted the history books and deprived my forefathers of their place in history? Why don't you understand the need for my children to discover the roots of their racial heritage? If you can be honest with yourself as you answer these questions, then there is hope for my children and your children in the next decade.

Along with my feelings of anger and hostility, there is a strong sense of disappointment. This disappointment is felt most keenly towards those who had taught me of God's love for all mankind. It was your missionaries who came to my native land with a message of love and mercy. When you brought me to your country against my will, you distorted God's words to justify your evil acts. You are still doing this, and I am still forbidden to attend some of your evangelical colleges and churches, and to be your neighbour. Do you think heaven will be segregated too?

Closely connected with this feeling of disappointment is a feeling of sorrow. I am deeply sorry that you have been misled in your thinking about me these many years. We both are suffering from this. You have missed out on many of the benefits of what I could have contributed, and now the financial burden of the black man is disturbing to you. Since you have deprived me of the right to develop my mind and reach my God-given potential, you have had to help me support my family. Yet out of this perhaps will come a better value-system. People are to be loved, not used. But now things are being loved, and people are being used. I feel that politicians usually do what is expedient, and that if Christians who know the love of God fail to do what is right and just, there is little hope for our country.

I have been referring to myself as the black man. But I still feel I have not been allowed to reach complete manhood. You have made me doubt my ability to compete with you intellectually, and you keep stunting this area of my life with inferior school-systems. You cannot doubt my ability to compete with you physically, however—and you have used this to put a feather in your cap and money in your pockets.

It is as if my first hundred years in your country were my infancy. I was dependent upon you and I obeyed you; but I did not receive nourishment from you that would enrich me or help me to grow. I was like a foster child, not knowing my parentage and kept from knowing it. You as my foster parents used and abused me; you gave me no love, but your discipline was severe. I still remember those years. If your foster child cries out 'I hate you', perhaps you can understand that he is expressing a feeling that he has been deeply wronged.

The second hundred years were my childhood. I grew into childhood despite the methods used to keep me an infant. I started to become aware of some of these methods. I saw more of the unfairness of your treatment of me. At times I would fight back, but for the most part I continued to play the role you as-signed to me. I soon learned that when I would cry out for justice, the rules became stricter, the punishment more severe. During those second hundred years I was a 'boy', and you constantly reminded me of that status.

Over the last hundred years, I progressed into the adolescent stage, and now I feel I am ready to emerge into adulthood. Don't call me 'boy' any longer, because I will no longer accept that label. Haven't you seen the evidence of my growth? I no longer accept what you say as gospel truth, and I am not afraid to tell you. I am finding and recognising my own identity and sense of worth. I desire to make it on my own, and I become disturbed when you tell me I'm rushing things—this process has been going on for *over three centuries now*. If God in his mercy allows the human race to exist, I shall achieve my full manhood in a few more years.

I am telling you these things because I do want you to know me. You have tried to observe me from afar while maintaining your myths and fantasies about me. I quote the following from a letter written by a young white person after a Christian conference where this problem was discussed:

Almost every white person I know who has been raised with prejudice and has come out of it, has done so because of a warm relationship with some Negro. This happened to me when I was seventeen, and I worked for a wonderful Negro man, who was one of the first persons I ever really loved and admired. Those who have not had this kind of experience frequently complain that they are paralysed in relating to those with the dark skin. If they try too hard, they create resentment by gushing and realise they aren't being very human. If they don't try, their old prejudices come out. They are unable to be friendly in a take-it-or-leave-it way.

The patterns of a lifetime are difficult to erase. Both you and I have blind spots. We both are indwelt with an innate depravity that without the constraining power and love of Christ can cause us to destroy ourselves as well as each other. We both are prone to anger, resentment, and hostility. Yet we both respond to love and acceptance and respect, and we both have the basic drives to live, to love, and to enjoy companionship. Our experiences are different, and I may consciously or unconsciously misinterpret your intentions initially, as you may misinterpret mine. Unfortunately, those of us in the older generation must learn again to give each other a chance, something we might have been willing to do when we were children if we had been allowed to.

I, the black man, suggest that you really get to know yourself. Evaluate your life experiences and see how they may have given you your views of the black man. The only real frontier we have on earth is the frontier of human relationships. Let us hope and trust that ultimately, as we have learned to release energy from the nucleus of the atom, we shall learn to release a greater energy from the nucleus of the soul. If that happens, it will enable us to love and to live together and enjoy the blessings God intended us to share.

Your fellow human being and future friend,
THE BLACK MAN

The roots of racism are imbedded deep within the life history of the individual as well as in the history of mankind. The term 'psychodynamics' refers to the systematised knowledge and theory of human behaviour and its motivations. Psychodynamics contends that a person's total make-up and probable reaction at any given moment are the product of past interaction between his specific genetic endowment and the environment, both animate and inanimate, in which he has been living from the time of his conception.

A child is born as free of racial prejudice as of political preference. The significant activities and needs of a human being are not determined by the amount of melanin in his skin. While the black man's and white man's experience in this society differs, the principle of physiological and psychological functions is the same. As William H. Grier and Price M. Cobb write:

There is nothing reported in the literature or in the experience of any clinician known to the authors that suggests that black people *function* differently psychologically from anyone else. Black man's mental functioning is governed by the same *rules* as that of any other group of men. Psychological principles understood first in the study of white men are true no matter what the man's colour (*Black Rage*, 1968, p. 129).

To understand the behaviour pattern of racism we must dig below the surface. The influence of the child's early thought-patterns stains his life-long perspective of his fellow human beings in ways of which he may not be conscious. Many white Bible-believing, evangelical Christians find it impossible to accept a black man into fellowship with them. Why?

We shall first examine how the emotional effects, attitudes, and concepts of colour lead to racial prejudice.

As the child's external sensory apparatus of sight and hearing develops, he is developing also the internal psychic mechanism. He does this through reflex behaviour, associations, assimulations, and various psychic defence mechanisms—processes that enable him to interpret the various images and concepts that are to be t part of his life. The significant adults in the child's life convey not only thought-patterns but their own anxieties. There is an intermingling of concrete and abstract stimuli, and emotional and ntellectual responses are formed.

At approximately the age of three or four, the child is becoming amiliar with the colour spectrum. While his eyes are interpreting and distinguishing colours, his ears are picking up various phrases. Pure and white', 'black as sin', 'yellow coward', 'savage redskins' —these are emotionally flavoured word concepts that portray colour as abstract qualities. Such phrases in the primitive thought patterns of the child's mind become emotionally charged by he various methods of reinforcing present in the child's environment.

One of those methods of reinforcement is fear, which may be used to control the child's behaviour. The child may be told that if you're bad the big black bogeyman will get you'. In this way he colour black can become 'phobogenic'. 'Phobia' is the term used to describe the process in which a fear becomes attached to objects or situations that objectively are not a source of danger. The object or circumstance selected to be feared is something that can be avoided. The child may fear his parents but is unable to avoid them. If he is told about the 'big black bogeyman', he is given an object of fear that he can avoid and repulse. This 'black object' can later become the first black boy he meets in kindergarten.

I vividly recall one of the first poems I heard recited to me during my kindergarten days:

> God made the nigger;
> He made him in the night,
> He made him in a hurry,
> He forgot to paint him white.

The five-year-old white boy who recited this to me had already been programmed to have a racist view of a fellow human being. To this child, at the age of five, colour had become a measure of a person's worth, and in his deception he attempted to make me an inferior creature of God.

The fantasy of white-good, black-bad, white-superior, black-inferior, has been maintained and preserved by our society with all the resources at its command. In the past, both Christians and non-Christians used pseudo-scientific articles to perpetuate the

41

fantasy. This method of brainwashing is seen in the following quotation:

> Before the abolition of slavery persons of mixed Negro and White were produced in very large quantities in the southern states. The best blood of the south flowed in the veins of Virginia and South Carolina slaves, and there is said to have been not a plantation in Louisiana on whose cotton fields there were not to be found the half-brothers, and half-sisters, the children or the grandchildren of the owners kept at work by the overseer's whip (Baur, Fisher, and Lenz, *Human Heredity*, third edition, 1931, p. 628).

What conclusion would you draw from this information? By a process of mental distortions, the author draws this one: 'Naturally this extensive admixture of white blood has contributed to raising the intellectual level of the coloured population.' And so amoral slave-owners who exploited the minds, bodies and souls of fellow human beings, disobeying the laws of God and man, are portrayed as if their sins were a blessing.

How can a white Christian who knows and believes the Bible refuse to have fellowship with his black brother? This is accomplished through a mechanism called logic-tight compartments. Arthur P. Noyes gives the following example:

> The psychotic patient may live simultaneously in two related worlds—one of fantasy, and one of reality. One patient in his fantasy would own the United States Treasury and its contents; he built and controlled the hospital in which he lived, but had just lost the key to it. Almost daily he would hand his physician an order for a billion dollars, at the same time begging for some tobacco and that he be given parole of the grounds. . . . This coexistence of the consciousness of fantasy and the consciousness of reality is made possible by the mechanism of rationalisation and its production of what is known as logic-tight compartments. Related ideas exist in each compartment undisturbed by those in the others, each group pursuing its course segregated from those which are incompatible, by a barrier through which no reassuring or argument can force a passage (*Modern Clinical Psychology*, fourth edition, p. 62).

Logic-tight compartments produced by the defence mechanisms of rationalisation and denial are not only found in the psychotic patient; they are also found in persons who are considered to be of sound mental health. By such a mechanism, a white Bible-believing Christian can read a verse such as 1 John 4:20—'If anyone says "I love God," and hates his brother, he is a liar . . .'—and refuse to have fellowship with his black brother.

Our society has been instrumental in planting the seeds of racism in other concepts besides colour. Dr. Charles A. Pinder-hughes tells how words such as 'high' and 'low' are used to assign roles to people:

> High-type people are associated in the mind with the high part of the body, with the head, with thinking, with leadership, with what is taken in and believed and with food. Low-type people are associated with the lower body, with the bottom, with the perineum, with what is excluded and expelled. Lower parties are often trained or moulded by upper parties and sent out on missions often as expendable, as reflected in military and other hierarchal organisations (*Journal of the American Psychiatric Association*, May 1969, p. 1552).

A person's behaviour is likely to be influenced by whether he is perceived, and in turn perceives himself, as 'high type' or 'low type'. This also determines whether he sees himself as one who should control or should be controlled. The systematic manner in which the black man has been held in the 'low' position perpetuated the fantasy that the black man was less human and less worthy than the white man, who made laws to enforce this fantasy. This paternalistic attitude of the white man towards the black man is reflected not only in political areas, but also in the missionary efforts of the Church.

Because our society is programmed to reproduce white power and not black power, the concept of black people being in positions of control has been difficult to accept. Forming a positive self-image is extremely difficult in the black community. The white child, on the other hand, through word concepts of colour and of 'high type' and 'low type', is inculcated with a sense of self-aggrandisement and control. Any challenge to his authority, whether violent or non-violent, must be suppressed.

Perhaps the most important dynamic factor determining personality is a person's choice of a device to handle his fears and anxieties. From his earliest existence, man has used the defence mechanism of projection—finding a scapegoat. Adam said to

God, 'The woman whom thou gavest to be with me, she gave me of the tree, and I did eat'. Like individuals, a society can project repressed impulses on to an outside source when its members learn to project the same impulses to a given object or an idea. By this process, group members identify with people who are perceived as similar ('our kind') and trustworthy; they are associated with the 'higher things of life', and thought of as right. Those who are different are perceived as objects not to be trusted but to be regarded with suspicion. Their culture may be strange; their appearance is unlike that of group members. They are considered either wrong or inadequate and must be rejected. They must be kept out of the 'In' group. Some of the ideas and thoughts of members of the 'In' group are delusions and fantasies, though they are not recognised as such because all the members believe them and use their reason and their other facilities to support them.

To act out impulses of anger or hostility on other members of the group would interfere with society's sense of unity, so the 'In' group finds an outside object on which to project those impulses. For more than 300 years, the black man has provided that scapegoat for white 'In' American society. He was, as could plainly be seen, different, and it was a difference he could not hide. To the black man could be conveniently imputed all those repressed, forbidden impulses our human nature harbours. The forbidden sexual impulses, for example, were placed upon him, and that projection gave rise to further myths and fantasies.

A weak society, like a weak individual, is threatened because of immature thinking processes; it neglects to build up an inner strength and instead builds outer defences that delude it into thinking it is strong. The process of segregation is such an outer defence, and it has been harmful to our country. Now the black man is saying to the white man, 'I am no longer going to be your scapegoat'. The young black child is not swallowing the poison that has tended to make him hate himself but is spitting it back into the faces of those whose forefathers fed it to his forefathers. Now that the psychological projections of the white man are not being accepted by the black man, white society is frantically searching for another scapegoat. Perhaps the hippies are fulfilling this role.

The Christian Church has tended to maintain society's fantasies by presenting a false picture of the Christ of the Bible. It has tended to portray Jesus as an Anglo-Saxon, blue-eyed, blond, Protestant (and, some add, Republican) Saviour. As William E. Pannell

44

writes in *My Friend the Enemy*, 'this conservative brand of Christianity perpetuates the myth of white supremacy'.

Underlying all injustices and the desire to dominate is the self-serving inner force that Freud called the 'Id'. The basic nature of man, which in theology we know as our sinful nature, cuts across all racial lines, and the black man as well as the white man is subject to this disease that perhaps more than any other causes one human being to dehumanise another. The Black Panthers—who refer to white policemen as pigs—have learned this lesson in dehumanisation well. So have white men who refer to blacks as monkeys or apes. When we deprive human beings of their humanity and soul, we can justify and rationalise anything we do to them. We can murder them, lynch them, or shoot them as easily as we shoot a squirrel or rabbit.

Perhaps the black man's use of the word 'soul' is a reminder to himself and his white brother that he is human, that he is a 'living soul'.

Race and the Local Church

STEPHEN F. OLFORD

Racism is a global problem. In every part of the world that I have travelled I have found this issue to be a burning one. In fact, in certain parts of Africa, I have encountered tribal hatred among people of the same colour and ethnic background. I have to confess, however, that some of the most ugly forms of racism are to be identified with our western world, especially in the United States of America and Britain.

Of course, the word 'race' is a term which is grossly misunderstood. As a black brother said to me on my television programme recently:

'I don't suppose there is a more loaded word . . . and yet it is a most imprecise word, for it is not even a technical word. Social scientists and anthropologists don't even know what the word means. Do we judge a person by the length of his nose, or the texture of his hair? What is our standard of evaluation? The whole matter of racism is so illogical and unreasonable, and when we view it from a biblical standpoint, it is utterly foreign to the heart of God. For this very reason, the Church has to be honest about this whole problem and, without fear or favour, must speak out against it. And there is only one vantage place from which we can proclaim the truth with authority, and that is the foot of the cross.'[1]

These sentiments were also impressively expressed by my dear friend, the Reverend Festo Kivengere of African Enterprise, when he discussed with me the hostility and enmity with which he has had to contend both in Africa and in the western world. He said with feeling and insight that Calvary was the only place of reconciliation.

'Only at the cross can we know a love which gives and forgives. Our example is our precious Lord who manifested both humility

46

and authority when he looked upon his murderers with infinite love and prayed, "Father, forgive them; for they know not what they do." His humility was demonstrated in his obedience, even to the death of the cross, while his authority was exhibited in making possible the absolution of the sins of his tormentors. It is true he asked his Father to forgive, but only on the basis of his own self-sacrifice.'

We cannot reflect upon these words of Mr. Kivengere without agreeing that *Calvary is the only place of reconciliation.*

Early in my pastoral ministry I came to see this fact, and therefore preached accordingly. Perhaps the passage that means more to me and to my members than I can ever express is 2 Corinthians 5:14–21. Paul tells us there that:

'the love of Christ constraineth us; because we thus judge, that if one died for all, then "all died" (ASV): and that he died for all, that they which live should not henceforth live unto themselves, but unto him which died for them, and rose again. Wherefore henceforth know we no man after the flesh: yea, though we have known Christ after the flesh, yet now henceforth know we him no more. Therefore if any man be in Christ, he is a new creature: old things are passed away; behold, all things are become new. And all things are of God, who hath reconciled us to himself by Jesus Christ, and hath given to us the ministry of reconciliation; to wit, that God was in Christ, reconciling the world unto himself, not imputing their trespasses unto them; and hath committed unto us the word of reconciliation. Now then we are ambassadors for Christ, as though God did beseech you by us: we pray you in Christ's stead, be ye reconciled to God. For he hath made him to be sin for us, who knew no sin; that we might be made the righteousness of God in him.'

If Calvary love means anything in the life of the local church, then it gives us, first, *God's conception of man.* So Paul says: 'Wherefore henceforth know we no man after the flesh: yea, though we have known Christ after the flesh, yet now henceforth know we him no more.' To be united with Christ in his death and resurrection is to gain new standards of judgment; new ways of looking at things. Knowing a man 'after the flesh' is to know him by the outward accidents and circumstances of life, such as his colour,

47

his culture, or his condition. But Calvary changes that whole conception of man. To strengthen his argument, Paul proceeds to affirm that even our judgment of Christ himself has to be totally altered by our understanding of what happened at Calvary. In the case of the Apostle, before he appreciated the passion of our Saviour, Christ was nothing more than a man who was born in obscurity, lived in restricted surroundings and died a humiliating death. Indeed, his evaluation of Jesus lead him to dismiss him as an impostor, and to persecute his followers. But after his conversion on the Damascas road, all was changed. Jesus was now the Redeemer of all men, for he had 'died for all'. From henceforth all men were equal, irrespective of colour, culture or condition. And Calvary means nothing to you or me if our view of man has not been similarly changed.

But in the second place, Calvary love gives us *God's creation in man*—'Therefore if any man be in Christ, he is a new creature: old things are passed away; behold, all things are become new.' Here the Apostle reaches a great climax in his reasoning. The regenerating experience that had taken place in his own life, because of the death and resurrection of Jesus Christ, could be equally possible in any other son of Adam's race. God had prophesied, through his servant Isaiah, that such a day would dawn when men would become new creatures in Christ Jesus (Isa. 43:18–19, 21).

So it is true to say, in the words of Professor Tasker: 'Every man regenerated by the Spirit of God is a new creation, and a world in which such creations exist is potentially, at least, a new world.'[2] In this new world there are no personal discriminations or racial tensions, for we are all 'the children of God by faith in Christ Jesus. For as many of (us) as have been baptized into Christ have put on Christ. There is neither Jew nor Greek, there is neither bond nor free, there is neither male nor female: *for (we) are all one in Christ Jesus*' (Gal. 3:26–8).

But there is a third aspect of this reconciling truth which works wonders in the local church. If we know Calvary love, we share *God's commission to man*. Paul reminds us: 'All things are of God, who hath reconciled us to himself by Jesus Christ, and hath given to us the ministry of reconciliation; to wit, that God was in Christ, reconciling the world unto himself, not imputing their trespasses unto them; and hath committed unto us the word of reconciliation. Now then we are ambassadors for Christ, as though God did beseech you by us: we pray you in Christ's stead, be ye reconciled to God. For he hath made him to be sin for us, who knew no sin; that we might be made the righteousness of God in him.' Our commission within the Body of Christ is to sense the burden and then to share the blessing of reconciliation. When we speak of the burden of this truth we are using biblical language. In Old Testament times this word was used again and again, especially by the prophets, to convey the thought of 'a heavy, weighty thing, or a message and oracle of God'. Isaiah speaks of 'the burden of Babylon, which Isaiah the son of Amoz did see' (Isa. 13:1). And in a similar fashion, the prophecy of Habakkuk opens with the words, 'The burden which Habakkuk the prophet did see' (Hab. 1:1).

This is what Paul is speaking of in the passage before us. He says: 'God . . . hath committed unto us the *word* of reconciliation.' God could remind Jeremiah in his day that 'every man's word shall be his burden' (Jer. 23:26). Some of us who know the responsibility of preaching understand exactly what this means. Every time we declare the 'word of reconciliation' we have to keep in mind both the proclamation and the invitation. The proclamation is that 'God was in Christ, reconciling the world unto himself, not imputing their trespasses'; and in order for this to be possible, he (God) 'made him (the Lord Jesus) to be sin for us, who knew no sin; that we might be made the righteousness of God in him'. Before sin, as an act or as a state or as a nature, could be dealt with, the Lord Jesus had to pay the penalty of being identified with sin. As John R. W. Stott puts it:

'Having been made flesh in the womb of Mary his mother, Christ was made sin on the cross of Calvary. God who would not impute our trespasses to us imputed them instead to Christ and made his sinless Son to be sin for our sake. How God could have been in Christ when he made Christ to be sin I cannot say. We are here touching the ultimate paradox of the atonement. But Paul taught both, and we hold both, even if we cannot satisfactorily reconcile them or neatly formulate them.'[3]

Here, then, is the burden of reconciliation that we must sense. Until the weight of God's mighty act in Christ is truly felt in our souls we have no word to preach and we have no world to reach.

But if Calvary means anything to us at all, not only do we sense the burden of reconciliation, but we are impelled to go forth and *share* the blessing of reconciliation. So Paul declares: 'Now then we are ambassadors for Christ, as though God did beseech you by us: we pray you in Christ's stead, be ye reconciled to God.' Professor Tasker reminds us that 'a minister of this word of reconciliation . . . can most probably be described as an ambassador for Christ, a title both *proud* and *humble*'.[4] In other words, our preaching of the message of reconciliation must be characterised by the authority and humility of Christ. Both these thoughts are embodied in this concept of the ambassador.

There must be, first, the authority of Christ. Hodge remarks that 'an ambassador is at once a messenger and a representative. He does not speak in his own name. He does not act on his own authority. What he communicates is not his own opinion or demands, but simply what he has been told or commanded to say. But at the same time he speaks with authority, and in this case the authority of Christ.' So we are to persuade men 'in Christ's stead (to) be . . . reconciled to God'. How anyone can speak in Christ's stead and be uncertain or apologetic about his message is hard to imagine!

But with the authority of Christ there is the humility of Christ — 'We are ambassadors for Christ, as though God did beseech you by us.' We are told that ambassadors are chosen especially for their tact, their dignity, their courtesy and persuasive powers. Ambassadors for Christ should show the same characteristics. This is why Paul says: 'I beseech you by the meekness and gentleness of Christ' (2 Cor. 10:1). Now to my mind, this distinctive element is lacking in our gospel preaching today. It is bad enough not to know the authority of Christ, but even worse not to exhibit the humility of Christ. In order to emphasise the importance of this manner of preaching the Apostle describes a pleading God beseeching men and women to be reconciled.

Alexander Maclaren captures this thought in a most moving passage in one of his sermons. He says:

'To sue for love, to beg that an enemy would put away his enmity is part of the inferior rather than that of the superior; is part of the offender rather than of the offended; is part of the vanquished rather than that of the victor; is the part surely not of the king but of the rebel. And yet here, in the sublime transcending of all human precedent and pattern which characterises the divine dealing, we have the place of the suppliant and of the supplicated inverted, and Love upon the throne bends down to ask of the rebel that lies powerless and sullen at his feet and yet is not conquered until his heart be won, though his limbs be manacled, that he would put away all the bitterness out of his heart, and come back to the love and grace which are ready to pour over him. "He that might the vengeance best have taken, finds out the remedy".'[5]

Here is humility indeed; and let it be observed that God longs to plead in this fashion in and through us day by day. And we do not fulfil our task of pastoral evangelism unless we preach with the authority and humility of Christ.

It was because of this understanding of 'pastoral evangelism' that I sensed the burden and shared the blessing of reconciliation with my church, which I have now served for thirteen years. When I came to Calvary Baptist Church in New York City, I was dismayed to learn that we had a segregated membership. Perhaps I had assumed too much when making inquiries about the new charge from a geographical point three thousand miles away! Of one thing I was immediately convinced: the situation had to be changed or else I could not remain pastor of this congregation. Needless to say, I prayed much about the matter and then began to study the problem in depth. I discovered that well over eighty-five per cent of the members were against integration. This presented an enormous challenge, and to make matters worse, I had outside powers pressing me to act immediately, or else! One black Federal judge came to see me because he was convinced that I was a racist. He reasoned that since I had not fought the issue, even to the point of splitting the church, I was not for integration. I pleaded with him to have patience, and explained that the answer to the problem would come through prayer, the preaching of the word of reconciliation, and the reviving of the Holy Spirit. Eventually he was persuaded when my secretary made him read one of my sermons on the race issue while he waited for an interview! Amazingly enough, that interview never took place. He studied the manuscript, returned it to my secretary and said, 'I am satisfied'. I never saw him again.

Days, weeks and months went by and I sensed a tremendous change of spiritual climate as the word of reconciliation was proclaimed with human weakness, to be sure, and yet with divine unction. In fact, such was the moving of God in our midst that the provisional dateline that I had set for a church meeting on the race issue was brought forward by six months. I shall never forget that night. Everybody was there, including several who should never have been present! I felt it my duty, on this occasion, to take a *personal* stand and not involve my officers, save as they spoke for themselves. Again, with a message bathed in prayer, I delivered my soul on this burning issue, expounding the Scriptures and fielding the questions from every part of the sanctuary. It is true that vitriolic language was used by some, and tense moments experienced by all; but when we came to the vote, the victory of our God was overwhelmingly evident. The vote was practically unanimous. Only eleven raised their hands in opposition. Of these eleven, seven assured me that while they did not see eye-to-eye with me on this matter, they were prepared to support the ministry 100 per cent. The remaining four were sovereignly removed from our midst in a manner which brought 'great fear' upon the church. One man died that very week!

I have often been asked how things have proceeded since then; and my answer, I am grateful to say, is always positive and triumphant. God has blessed us beyond all our asking or thinking. Even though we have had the problems that are common to any inner-city church, the question of integration has not been one of them. We have found that the people who have sought the right hand of fellowship at Calvary are those who are prepared to submit themselves to the discipline and training of our membership classes, and have, as a consequence, accepted the standard of ministry, the manner of worship, and the opportunities for service as structured within our church. In this connection, we have black brethren and members of other minority groups represented on our boards, committees, the choir, and similar organisations—all working *together* for the glory of God. Sometimes I feel that Calvary Church is like a little Pentecost, for every Sunday there are people from so many nations under heaven! At our Visitors' Reception not so very long ago, there was a roll call, and it was noted that no less than forty-six different countries across the world were represented in that particular worship service!

Praise the Lord, we have learned that *integration comes through reconciliation*; and that reconciliation takes place at the foot of the cross when 'red and yellow, black and white' are prepared to be broken and mastered by the constraining love of Christ.

1. Interview with Bill Pannell, Associate Evangelist, Tom Skinner Crusades on 'Encounter', May 4 1969

2. R. V. G. Tasker, *2 Corinthians*. The Tyndale New Testament Commentaries (London, Tyndale Press), p. 88

3. John R. W. Stott, *The Preacher's Portrait* (London, Tyndale Press, 1961), p. 42

4. R. V. G. Tasker, op. cit. p. 89

5. *Expositions of Holy Scripture* (Grand Rapids, Eerdmans Publishing House), Vol. 9, p. 382

Missions and Race

ERNEST OLIVER

J. H. Oldham in his book *Christianity and the Race Problem* (SCM, London, 1924) fearlessly sets out the facts and causes of racial antagonism, and it probably still represents the best thinking of the missionary movement on racism.

It has been assumed that the missionary movement contributed largely towards the breaking down of racial barriers, but no serious discussion has taken place on whether Missions and missionaries were themselves purveyors of racist attitudes and practices.

The communication of the Christian message to the whole world was the task committed to the disciples by the Risen Christ. The Acts of the Apostles begins with a reiteration of the worldwide commission and records the fulfilment of it to the Mediterranean lands as far as Rome.

It was plain that this commission involved crossing geographical frontiers and Christian missionaries showed little hesitation about accepting the implications of wide travelling for the sake of the gospel. But when Paul and Barnabas returned from their first journey with stories of the conversion of Gentiles the Church had to face as a body what Peter had faced individually when he set off to preach to the house of Cornelius. Racial frontiers, too, had to be crossed and crossed not in a patronising manner. There could be no 'dogs eating the crumbs that fall from the master's table' attitude about giving the gospel to non-Jewish people. The Council at Jerusalem took a crucial decision about Gentile converts reporting Peter's own words about being saved by faith, but Peter's own behaviour at Antioch (Gal. 2:11–14) manifested a racist attitude in spite of non-racist principles.

Pokhail John George of the Mar Thoma Syrian Church wrote an article in the *International Review of Missions*, July 1970, entitled 'Racist Assumptions of the nineteenth century Missionary Movement'. The assumptions he says were inevitable when the movement 'was a one way affair from the rich dominant modern societies of the West to the ancient or primitive but dominated societies of Asia, Africa and Latin America', and when the missionaries believed they 'were equipped with superior morals and cultures and that the people to whom they were going had inferior morals and culture'.

Missionaries have not only a great urge to reach every man with the gospel but are also convinced that we 'are all one in Christ Jesus'. It would be true to say that the Church all over the world owns a common allegiance to Jesus Christ and accepts equality in the family of God. The missionary has seen many things as obstacles to the spread of the gospel and the establishing of the worldwide Church which would bring all people to a common allegiance to Christ and therefore to an equality based on that allegiance. In his efforts to spread the gospel the missionary has fought with disease and ignorance, he has lifted men and women out of the subjection which is the lot of the poor and the un-educated, he has provided a way of deliverance from the fear of evil spirits and given a hope of eternal security and bliss. Perhaps more than any other category of men and women the missionary has prepared the people of subject nations for the day of political freedom. Men like Presidents Nyerere and Kaunda owe the opportunity to develop their great abilities to the Mission schools and colleges. Saintly men like C. F. Andrews inspired and in-structed many Indian leaders. People without a written language learned to communicate with paper and pen through the persis-tent labours of missionaries. Such has been the standard of devotion to their cause on the part of the missionaries, the practical expression of their love for the downtrodden and diseased, the willingness to lay down their lives rather than quit the field, that in pre-independence India the Indian National Congress leaders called for the showing of 'a missionary spirit' on the part of zealots and workers. But the missionary has generally not seen racism as an obstacle. After all he has given up everything to serve the people of another race, and on that basis alone he would feel that he could not be called a racist. Nationalism was certainly seen as an obstacle, and I remember being warned against Christian workers in India who were ardent nationalists. Many missionaries regarded any political expression on the part of the national brethren as evidence of a lack of real spiritual purpose.

While it is true to quote Ronald Segal in *The Race War*, that 'the Treaty of Nanking (1842) with subsequent agreements, prised China open to Western enterprise' and among numerous other things 'enforced formal agreement to the activities of Christian missionaries and converts throughout the country' it would be wrong to swallow unsuspectingly Pokhail George's contention that

> 'the missionaries made no effort to speak out against the oppressions of colonialism, while at the same time with confident assumption of moral superiority, they tried to make headway against the "darkness and idolatry" of the heathen world. . . . Both by omission (in not having a prophetic voice on behalf of the oppressed) and by commission (by supporting the colonial administrations) they had participated in institutional racism. They assisted in every effort to extend the Kingdom of God through the extension of Empires.'

The Protestant Mission in the Congo in 1903 raised their voices strongly against the 'rubber atrocities' perpetrated by King Leopold of the Belgians. They helped to organise the Congo Reform Association which determined to bring to an end this terrible oppression of a subject people. The *Regions Beyond* of October 1904 writes of its missionaries, 'whilst at the present moment much time must be given to the relief of the Congolese from outward oppression, the still greater work of teaching them the way of salvation continues to demand strenuous efforts and most constant prayer'. Missions have not been silent or inactive in similar instances of oppression in other parts of the world. The problems of Missions in Southern Africa are immense and by and large the interdenominational societies at work there have kept themselves apart from the political struggles in order to be allowed to continue their ministry to white and coloured people alike. Many missionaries would declare themselves in favour of the policies of separate development of the white and coloured people while others seem to have learned to live with a situation they feel they cannot change, even though they consider the extreme racial policies of South Africa to be abhorrent.

A lot has been written about 'missionary imperialism' both from the viewpoint of an imperialism that is missionary in 'that it does not even permit . . . peoples to live their own lives, to worship their gods, and to preserve their institutions and customs' (Klaus Knorr: *British Colonial Theories 1570–1850*), and from the viewpoint of the missionary who 'hoped to see the Yangtse Valley incorporated into the British Empire as a step towards civilisation' (John Kent *The History of Christian Missions in the Modern Era*).

There can be no doubt that missionary societies sought to work

peaceably and effectively within the established law and administration of the country. The British missionary in India was glad
to take advantage of the facility of entrance and movement afforded
to him by the British Raj, but in spite of strong denials he was
inevitably associated with the British Government and it was
therefore assumed that his work of preaching and teaching
Christianity was part of the British imperialist programme. One
day the missionary would set up his camp in a village and after
a few days move on. A few days later the District Collector would
set up his camp and collect the taxes. They were both regarded
as part of the same system.

It was often far harder for me as a missionary in British India
to bear the reproach of the British Crown than the reproach of
the Cross of Christ. We were fully expected to leave India after
August 1947, when India became independent, and the fact that
we did not went some way to dispel the idea of the imperialist
missionary. While the study of the growth of missions as a corollary
to colonial expansion is very interesting and certainly has an
important place among the many contributing factors, the accepted assumption that the missionary felt he possessed superior
morals and culture and went to people who had inferior morals
and culture had a far greater influence upon the results of the
nineteenth-century missionary movement than that of the supposed privileges of colonialism. Whereas colonialism in a political
sense at least has come to an end, the problems of 'race' or
'ethnocentrism' continue to plague the right relationships between
missions and churches all over the world.

George Seavers in his *David Livingstone: His Life and Letters 1957*
writing of Livingstone's friendship with Sechele, paramount chief
of the Bakwena said:

'Livingstone was himself an unusual exception to men of
European blood, in that he never felt conscious in Africa of
the colour bar. Sechele was unusual in his comprehension of
European modes of thought. But the existence of a natural
affinity between a white man and a black, recognised by each
of them from the first as mutual, is something that escapes the
bounds of ethnic psychology. On Sechele's side it stood the test
of many a strain imposed by his white friend's rigorist demands
in matters of faith and morals.'

By way of contrast to this is the candour of the Rev. Gabriel

57

M. Setiloane, former Youth Secretary of the All Africa Conference of Churches.

'This Missionary contempt for the "natives", I discovered later, was not restricted to those in Africa. It was a world illness: I met it in India, in the Salvation Army hostel where I stayed in Calcutta, in the Philippine Islands, in Singapore and far round the world in Mexico. They always talked about the despicable side of the life of the "natives". . . . It was all the same, "You cannot trust them", "You must keep everything locked up", "They are lazy, sensuous and immoral". And in the Church "the leaders jostle for power which they use for their own private ends".'

How indeed have missions handled this very sensitive area of their operations? In its report *Commission on World Mission—One World, One Task—1971*, the Evangelical Alliance said 'So far we have not directly mentioned something which has moved in and out of all the factors we have mentioned. It is potentially the most explosive factor of all—race. And perhaps its most disturbing feature is its "accidental" character.' Nowhere is it a more disturbing feature than in the life and activities of the Church throughout the world.

Gustav Warneck (1834–1910) the German Lutheran theologian who was deeply involved in the German Rhenish Mission's work among the Bataks in Sumatra, which was said to be 'the crowning achievement of Protestant Missions in the Dutch East Indies', believed in the colonial mission of the Europeans. The Europeans, he thought, were called to lead the coloured people out of their alleged cultural, economic and religious backwardness. He believed these people started with the handicap of an all but ineradicable racial weakness, and that their only hope of progress was in being led by the Europeans, especially the Germans with their emphasis on good order and discipline. From 1861 the Batak Mission succeeded in Christianising a whole nation, but it is ironical that the problems of partnership between Mission and Church had not been solved when the Second World War broke out in 1939 and the Church was suddenly deprived of its German leaders who were interned.

I have quoted this example as it demonstrates a conviction that was clearly held by the missionaries and they made no apology for formulating and acting upon policies based on that conviction.

Johannes Warneck, the son of Gustav Warneck said in 1934 after he had become Director of the Rhenish Mission Board in Germany

> 'It needs courage to risk the step of granting autonomy to the young Church. We must trust that God can do his work not only through the missionaries but also through the weak and struggling Church. In spite of all her mistakes and lapses we must trust the young Church, must believe that the Holy Spirit will guide her. All kinds of events might occur which might force the missionaries to leave. In that case the Batak Christians must be ready to take the helm.'

To what extent has this conviction been generally held by western missions, even though it may not have been stated so explicitly? How much has 'paternalism' really been 'racism' on the assumption of superior morals and culture? The 'accident' of race has indeed intruded upon the setting up and maintaining of right relationships throughout the worldwide church.

Joseph P. Fitzpatrick SJ, Professor of Sociology in Fordham University New York writes: (IRM July 1970)

> 'Once people of a particular culture have identified their own way of life with nature, they tend to judge other cultures according to the standards which prevail in their own. They tend to define as wrong or evil or unnatural the cultural practices which constitute the way of life of peoples of a culture different from their own ... Once the people of one culture have defined their way of life as 'natural', and it is inevitable that they will do so, once they have begun to define the way of life of others as wrong or unnatural, the possibility of communication is limited ... Basically, this is the problem of what has come to be called 'racism' today. Sociologists and anthropologists have always called it 'ethnocentrism', the tendency to judge other people by their own culture, to judge them according to the norms which prevail in my way of life rather than their own.'

It is significant that in his analysis of the causes of the growth of the Independent African Church Movement, David Barrett (*Schism and Renewal in Africa*) has discovered the highest incidence of independence to be related to the existence of colonialism, the large concentration of foreign missionaries and the availability of the whole Bible in the vernacular. In other words 'independence' (and we are not admitting a Scriptural authority for all the multivarious forms of independence throughout Africa) has sprung up largely through the clash of cultures and the freedom to interpret the Scriptures in accordance with their own culture on the part of millions of African Christians.

Missionary societies have encouraged the establishment of 'national' missionary societies as 'points of concentration' for extensive evangelism by the churches. 'The Million Souls Movement' in Korea in 1909 and 1910 and the Kongsi Batak of the Batak Church in Sumatra founded in 1899 were examples of this and the majority of churches in Asia, Africa and Latin America have similar organisations. But it was very rarely that 'nationals' were admitted into the 'missionary' fellowships of the societies. Some societies did experiment with the inclusion of 'national' missionaries as did the RBMU in India between the years 1930 and 1945. For a church-planting society with an organisation separate from the churches, however, the 'national missionary' supported by foreign funds on scales far in excess the church leaders, was thought to be a hindrance and the practice was abandoned.

If the missionary society is intent on remaining organisationally separate from the churches then it would appear to disqualify itself from including within its ranks the local Christian workers. While it is possible that racial factors may sometimes be hidden within the decision of the missionary society to remain separate from the churches, the non-inclusion of national Christian workers in a missionary society is not generally to be regarded as racial discrimination. The place of the national Christian workers is within the local church organisation and administration.

A number of the denominational societies have always admitted Christian workers from Asia and Africa into their missionary fellowship, both as direct appointees and also as the husbands and wives of the missionaries from their sending countries. It is only recently, however, that inter-denominational societies have changed their declared or implicit policies on the admission of Asian, African or Latin American workers to their strictly 'caucasian' fellowships. In 1965 for instance the Overseas Missionary Fellowship became a truly international missionary fellowship with its headquarters in Singapore. The only stipulation being that an Asian would be a missionary to a country other than his own. Similarly the Bible and Medical Missionary Fellowship has Asian members in its work in the Indian sub-continent.

It does appear, however, that the image of the white-dominated mission organisation will remain, even with the significant changes already mentioned, until there is a general acceptance of complete integration into the churches overseas. Until that happens policies of separation based on such things as freedom to continue the task of evangelism, or non-interference in the life and administration of the churches will always be suspected as racial in essence, and for this reason alone I believe they should be faced honestly and squarely.

It would be quite wrong to conclude that in general the work of missions throughout the past 180 years has been less successful than it could have been because of 'ethnocentrism'. In great areas of the world the seed of the Word has produced churches related to the soil of the countries to which missionaries went. Many churches in Korea, Indonesia, Nigeria, as well as Latin America have shown their tremendous vitality in the Spirit in the dissemination of a faith in Jesus Christ that is wholly assimilable within the local culture. The Holy Spirit has done his work and no one has been more delighted than the missionary when he has seen the Church break out from the limitations which he has inadvertently set because of his own culture and religious background.

Race and the Overseas Student

WILLIAM K. VIEKMAN

It is appropriate that this chapter follows the one entitled
'Missions and Race', for the two are directly related. Not since
Pentecost have so many travelled so far and to so many foreign
lands, to study and to gain understanding of alien cultures. Never
have so many intermingled and sought answers to delicate
questions concerning race relations. The student world is alive
with open discussions on sensitive, previously closed issues having
to do with racial harmony. To pass immediately to Christian
considerations, a vital definition must be made here. The evangelical church speaks of 'the mission field', using the term as a
geographical expression. It is strongly urged that 'the mission field'
be understood rather to refer to *people*. Thus the 'field' of Peru
means Peruvian citizens in their homeland—or Peruvian nationals
strolling on State Street in Chicago, Illinois. In the Christian
context, then, the believers in each nation are responsible for
befriending people of other countries for the sake of Jesus Christ.
Why? The students will one day graduate, and return home with
fixed attitudes about their education, the western world in general
and, most specifically, about Jesus Christ. We are, therefore, in
the midst of one of the most dynamic opportunities for evangelising
the world since that long ago day of Pentecost in the book of Acts.
There the Church was commissioned and commanded to preach
the gospel *to* all the world—*in* all the world—beginning at
Jerusalem. Yet it must not be lost sight of that our sovereign God,
as Lord of History, brought the world, that is, *people*, 'from every
nation under Heaven' right to Jerusalem, and there made his
power apparent to them. The initial 3,000 international converts
remained in Jerusalem (Acts 2:42) studied Bible doctrine, enjoyed
fellowship, broke bread and grew in grace with each prayer
meeting. Then, in Acts 8:4, along with other Jerusalem Christians
no doubt, they went *everywhere* (where they had come from),
'preaching the word'. While this order of historical events must
not be made into a doctrine (Acts is an historical book), it is

becoming clearer with each passing day that we in the 1970's are in the very midst of experiencing identical spiritual aspects of this cycle. People from overseas are here with us—now!

The intermingling of the races of the world, has been made possible by rapid air transportation and a wide diffusion of knowledge. This communication between races, temporary though its basis may be, is of vast significance on six counts:

First, in the area of strategy: for many centuries, the Church of Jesus Christ has obediently sought to go—that is, to send white men—to the other races of the world carrying to them the life-giving message of the gospel. The success of the Church's mission is evident in the many congregations now worshipping Christ throughout Asia, in the hinterlands of Latin America, and in the very heart of Africa. However, there are places where the western Church has never been permitted to go. There are lands which have never opened the door to the Christian message, and are still closed in this final quarter of the twentieth century. International travel, on the other hand, has opened to us a new door—one which no man can shut. This opening, this intermingling of races and cultures represents an exciting development, for it affords a fresh opportunity for Christians to share their love and faith with those who come from other nations, even 'closed' ones. The potential is truly exciting. I recall a man who came from a 'closed' land, who saw and heard of the love of Jesus Christ and was so deeply moved that he himself became a believer before he left for home. He went back to a difficult place—a land to which no foreign missionary could go. He is there today, and has already become an effective witness to his own people.

There has been among foreign students a common misunderstanding—that of feeling that Christianity is basically an American, or Western, or White Man's religion. The truth of the matter is that the Bible is more readily understandable (culturally) to an Oriental. For example, the Japanese fully comprehend the 'May your servant find grace in your sight' of the Old Testament. They themselves have reduced the expression to just two words—'Dōzo yoroshiku'. It is, after all, a near eastern, and thus an oriental, concept. So it goes with much of the Bible's cultural setting.

Actually, the fascinating thing to share with other cultures and races is that biblical Christianity is unique because it is not a religion at all, but a *dynamic*. Everlasting life is not something gained by human works, but given as a gift by Jesus Christ—given *freely* to all who personally accept him. Furthermore, it is exciting to share with other cultures, with other races, the truth that biblical Christianity will never be embraced by the world's majority, but by what the Bible calls a 'remnant' of people—a distinct minority. The idea then, is to share this dynamic with international students and visitors, particularly on a cross-cultural, cross-racial basis. That is, the western Christian should emphasise contacts with Africans, Asians and those with non-Christian backgrounds, being fully aware that in so doing the gospel of Christ will thereby enter even those lands hitherto referred to as 'closed'. So much for the out-and-out strategy.

Secondly, the presence of people of other races in our midst has solved a mathematical problem of long standing. While the word 'remnant' (Rom. 11:5) makes direct reference to spiritual Israel, it is a historical fact that Christians are in a minority in the world today. Whether in England, continental Europe or the United States those who truly know Jesus Christ are a remnant of people. When missionaries are sent out they become, in turn, a remnant from within a remnant—a very tiny minority indeed. This mathematical insufficiency has long plagued the Church. However, when our attention is turned to the opportunities that exist today, the chances of meeting people from overseas who are in our midst, men of other cultures and races, we must recognise immediately that every Christian has the opportunity, nay, the responsibility, to befriend the foreign visitor.

Students are very inquisitive. They travel far from home in order to learn something. Their minds are open intellectually and many of them have open hearts—a spiritual receptivity. The opportunity to reach these people is one of great significance. If this open door involves every believer (and of course no two Christians are exactly alike) what a vast potential for winning the hearts of those from foreign lands! But how can every Christian possibly qualify as an international missionary to these visiting students? Didn't foreign missionaries study for years to make the grade? True. The difference, however, is in the need of 'the fields that have come to us'. The greatest longing of the overseas student is for friendship—beginning with someone just to talk to, someone with whom to share a common 'wavelength'. Since every Christian has his own profession, speciality, hobby, or 'wavelength', everyone has a God-given ability to reach out to a counterpart from overseas. The greatest pre-requisite for this work, then, is simply that the Christian should be himself—and be concerned enough to get involved. Therefore, this operation on a common 'wavelength' affords the bridging of the most difficult gap in all missionary work—that of effectively making an initial contact.

We recall a man who came to our home from Japan. He was stopping only briefly, and we were to have the pleasure of his company for only one week. Yet for all of that time he was fairly bursting with questions—including deeply spiritual ones. He confessed that he was searching for the truth. In our guest room, on the very last day of his visit, he gave his heart to Jesus Christ. Just one week! We were astounded. In terms of immediate follow-up we had the opportunity only to equip him with a Japanese Bible before he went from us, and from our nation. Yet that man today, as a professor in a Japanese university, is sharing his faith in Christ with multitudes of young students, and is doing so in the context of his sociology lectures. Thus, since every Christian can potentially be available to the visitors from overseas, the gospel can thereby go into many areas of the world. This is a remarkable opportunity. This is something to be enthusiastic about because it is beautifully solving a mathematical problem—the perennial shortage of missionaries.

The third significance of this new, open door is an economic one. It has been difficult for the western Church to pay the bills for evangelising the world. Sending out a missionary is a very expensive proposition. What is involved is lengthy (and costly) intellectual training, equipment, transportation, repatriation funds, money for language study and the cost of support in an alien society. On the other hand, when a student from overseas has experienced the love of the Saviour through Christian friendship, and has personally accepted Christ, he returns to his homeland and spreads the Good News among his own countrymen, as the Holy Spirit directs him. It has been my privilege to travel to many nations following up these former visitors and to discover that wherever the new Christians have gone there has been a faithfulness to God, a desire for greater knowledge from his word and a sincere effort to make Christ known to fellow countrymen. And yet, prior to returning to their own nations, they did not ask the church in England, or the United States, for any funds. They did not make any demands upon western believers for passage, support, or language study monies. They simply returned home.

One is reminded again of Acts chapter 8 verse 4 where we read of the persecution that came to the believers in Jerusalem, who went everywhere 'preaching the Word'. Among those who fled from Jerusalem, were, no doubt, the 3,000 foreigners who had come to Christ back in Acts 2 at Pentecost. They simply went back home. May the western Church firmly grasp the significance of this.

The fourth meaningful factor is so vast, and so exciting, that it is almost beyond description. We are told that there are 2,796 languages in the world. There has therefore been, and still is, a great need for translators to go among the 'primitive' tribes of this earth to reduce the spoken word to writing. It must be clearly affirmed here that the mission of the Church of Jesus Christ remains a *total* effort involving home, foreign, and international forces. Men must still journey to the more inaccessible areas, from which people are not yet travelling to the western world. In our generation, however, many of the 2,796 languages have been reduced to one. No matter where our visitors come from they are the foreigners, they are the aliens, they are the ones who must learn *our* language. Therefore, it is possible to reach many of the nations of the earth with one language—English—when spoken slowly and distinctly. It is now possible to make Christ known internationally, to express the love which is characteristic of the gospel, and to demonstrate that love in one's *own* language. One can be himself, in his own home, speak his own tongue, yet share what God has to say to the nations. He can discuss questions relevant to the differences between the races. In short, in one language, it is now possible to entertain most of the world, and to share that which will definitely be re-echoed in the nations of the earth. This priceless message will go back, however, in the national languages spoken by our visitors.

An illustration of this is the visit which I enjoyed to a remote people in the Himalayan region. I did not speak one word of their tongue. I went seeking a former overseas student who had been particularly close to me, a man who had given his heart to the Lord Jesus Christ and who, from the beginning, expressed a strong desire to make the message of life known to his own people. I reached his country, found him, and enjoyed a priceless time of fellowship. I sought to encourage him in the Scriptures. We had prayer together, and he reiterated his determination to be a faithful missionary to the citizens of his country. And yet everything we shared was said in English. I still do not speak a single word of his language.

The fifth significant fact has to do with social strata. When my wife and I went to Japan as resident missionaries, we were soon told it would be quite simple to reach the grandmothers and children of the area in which we were to work. We were informed however, that the business man would be away at work and would come home only to eat and sleep, and that it would be extremely difficult to reach Japanese with the gospel on the complete family level. What could be said then for contacting high-placed families *at all*! In Matthew chapter nineteen it was the rich young ruler's great possessions that led him to reject Jesus. It has always been difficult to reach the upper strata of people in any society. And yet, this is the *very* group that is now coming in ever-increasing numbers to the western world. Here is a solid reason for the Church of Jesus Christ, for every Christian, to be willing to reach out, with a spirit of genuine friendship, to gain the confidence of the various races and cultures in our midst. That shy black man from Africa may become the Prime Minister of his country. That gentle and quiet Asian may one day be the leading banker of his nation. Let it be remembered that the present king of Thailand studied in Boston, Mass. Let it be known that many of the men now in Africa's leadership studied in London, England. The son of the King of Nepal is presently studying in the United States. And, surely, there are many men in the commercial leadership of Asia and Africa who have sent their children to study in the United Kingdom. Never has the Church had a greater opening in the cross-cultural and cross-racial dimension.

One example may suffice to reflect this truth respecting social strata. When President H. W. Guffey of International Students, Inc. visited some ex-foreign students in Africa, he was prepared to stroll the sidewalk with them as he had in America. He found himself, however, in the position of the honoured guest of a high official. He was ushered to a limousine that had awaited him at the airport, and was treated with dignity and respect because of the love that he had shown to that particular black man when he had studied for a time in the United States.

How can the Church take advantage of the presence of international students on its very doorstep? In terms of procedure there are three crucial words that must be memorised, words which will enable the Christian in the western world to be effective in communicating Christ on the cross-racial, cross-cultural level. These words are: friendship, confidence, and witness. These are strategic words, for friendship must be genuine, on the deepest level, the type of friendship that will earn confidence. Such confidence is necessary before there can be an effective witness. Unless there is an *initial* contact on the cross-cultural and cross-racial basis, there can be no meaningful sharing of the gospel of Christ. Never before in history has there been such an open door to reach people on the higher social levels. In order to win them, however, there must be a breaking down of racial animosity, of barriers which, in times past, have identified the white man with supremacy, and people of other races with inferiority. Only the demonstrated love of Christ can, and *will*, remove these stumbling blocks.

There is one more meaningful facet to this open door, a factor highly relevant in modern times. For many years the Asian and the black man have thought of Christianity as being a western religion. This vast mistake has caused deep misunderstanding, both racial and cultural. Yet, any meaningful study of the Bible will show that it is for *all* people. It is, as already stated, a document far easier for an oriental to understand culturally, than the modern, western citizen. To confuse biblical Christianity with mere religion is sad enough, but to identify it racially with the white man's world, is to flirt with sheer tragedy. Yet, in this very respect, the priceless opening before us calls for a living demonstration of a love that never fails to amaze the non-white, non-western, non-Christian world. It speaks of a vibrant experience which places the word of God (without apology) into the no-man's-land of racial and cultural conflict.

Biblical Christianity is a dynamic which does more than merely jump over cultural and racial barriers. It completely shatters them. Its message, when demonstrated by life and language, is guaranteed to evoke a response. This never fails. God himself made the promise in Isaiah 55:11a when he said, 'So shall my word be that goeth forth out of my mouth. It shall not return unto me void'. The Church of Jesus Christ in the space age has every reason to pursue with enthusiasm every possible contact with international students, businessmen, diplomats, military personnel, tourists, technicians and medical people on a cross-cultural and cross-racial basis.

The opportunities are here *now*. It is high time for the western Church to awake out of sleep.

Inter-Racial Marriage

DAVID W. TRUBY

While immigration is no new phenomenon, the twentieth century is seeing a vast, worldwide movement of peoples aided by increasing knowledge of conditions in other lands and by easy travel facilities. For example, in West Germany there are one million foreign workers, in France one and a half million, and in Switzerland one in every three employed persons is a foreigner. In Belgium some mines would cease operating without foreigners for they constitute eighty per cent of the labour force. Haitians are emigrating to the United States of America, Japanese to Brazil, Britons to Australia, New Zealand and Canada. Only three large groups of immigrants have come to the United Kingdom in the last century: people from Eastern Europe in the period preceding World War I, Jewish, Polish and other refugees in the periods before and after World War II, and a recent movement from the Commonwealth countries. It is this last group, which has settled, adapted to the British way of life and whose children are growing up and getting married, with whom this chapter is primarily concerned. Many immigrants have found their way into British churches, though unhappily many more have become influenced by current religious antipathy and have put aside church affiliation. But the fact remains that the latter teen-age group is seeking marriage, and when an attachment is formed between an immigrant and a traditional resident there are frequently criticisms both from parents and Christians, particularly if there is a difference of colour. It is our purpose to examine the question of inter-racial marriage from the Scriptures, from expediency and from experience.

INTER-RACIAL MARRIAGE IN THE OLD TESTAMENT

At first sight it may appear that inter-racial marriage is not approved in the Old Testament.

The deepening wickedness of man

Genesis 6:2 'The sons of God saw the daughters of men that they were fair; and they took them wives of all which they chose.'

Genesis chapter 6 records the increasing wickedness on the earth, which was to lead up to judgment by the Noahic Flood, and the 'wickedness' is introduced by the charge that the sons of God were marrying the daughters of men. Probably by the former is meant the family of Seth, who were religious, and by the latter the descendants of the apostate Cain. Marriages between parties of opposite principles and practice were a source of corruption: but the criticism of marriage here is on moral grounds, not racial.

The massacre of the Hivites (Genesis 34:1–31)
Although only about fifteen years of age, Dinah, of the tribe of Israel, had been associating with the men of the Hivite clan, and was abducted by them, according to Josephus, after a festival. Hamor, of the Hivites and father of the men responsible for her defilement, approached the sons of Jacob making an offer of peace through inter-racial marriage. (Verse 9) 'And make ye marriages with us, and give your daughters unto us, and take our daughters unto you.' This was an effort to unite the two peoples. The sons of Jacob agreed provided that the Hivites submitted to circumcision—the honour of their family depended upon it. The outward rite could not make Hivites true Israelites, and yet it does not appear that Jacob's sons required anything more. Nothing is said of their teaching the people to worship the true God, all they insisted on was the rite of circumcision, 'then will we give our daughters unto you, and we will take your daughters to us, and we will dwell with you, and we will become one people' (verse 16). A formal marriage of Dinah never took place, nor did the union of the two races, for the sons of Jacob fell upon the males of the Hivites and slaughtered them. Again the issue was a moral one. Their motive was revenge for dishonouring their sister, rather than showing aversion to inter-racial marriage.

The revelation of the law (Deuteronomy 7)
As the people of Israel advanced towards the Promised Land, God, through Moses, began revealing his Law. The Hivites, Hittites, Girgashites, Amorites and several other tribes were to be dispossessed of the land and Israel was to take it as a divine inheritance. The command of God regarding intermarriage with the other tribes was clear and concise, 'Neither shalt thou make marriages with them; thy daughter thou shalt not give unto his son, nor his daughter shalt thou take unto thy son' (Deuteronomy 7:3). Intermarriage would have two effects. First, there was the

danger that the religion of Israel would become tainted with pagan and animistic religion. Secondly, intermarriage would upset the 'balance of the tribes'. Therefore intermarriage is not just barred on grounds of race. There is a religious reason against the practice.

The reformation under Nehemiah

'In those days also saw I Jews that had married wives of Ashdod, of Ammon, and of Moab: and their children spake half in the speech of Ashdod, and could not speak in the Jews' language, but according to the language of each people. And I contended with them, and cursed them, and smote certain of them, and plucked off their hair, and made them sware by God, saying, Ye shall not give your daughters unto their sons, nor take their daughters unto your sons, or for yourselves.' (Nehemiah 13:23–25)

The historical situation was that Nehemiah heard of the plight of his people—and went to Jerusalem to see for himself. He surveyed the scene, saw the unfinished walls and Temple and then animated the people into action. In spite of opposition and intrigue he completed the task. It was then that he endeavoured to rebuild the 'inner Temple' of the people by publicly reading the Law and expounding it and by introducing reforms. He particularly emphasised the 'sin' of intermarriage with other tribes (chapter 13, verse 25). Again the problem was basically moral—when Jews married pagans then religion declined—and Nehemiah attributed the nationwide spiritual decline to intermarriage.

Three instances of inter-racial marriage in the Old Testament

In the Old Testament there are several instances of marriages between races. These are Moses with Zipporah, Solomon with Pharaoh's daughter and Ruth with Boaz. It is interesting to note that the first finds favour in the sight of God and the second is condemned, and it is profitable to examine the reason. Moses, after killing an Egyptian, fled in order to save his life, to Midian where he was befriended by a Midianite shepherd and his clan. 'And Moses was content to dwell with the man: and he gave Moses Zipporah his daughter' (Exodus 2:21). It would seem, however, that Zipporah accepted Moses' faith in the one true God, even though she complained bitterly at having to circumcise their child (Exodus 4:25). The fact remains that this marriage did not deter God from using Moses, and he was in fact appointed to plead before Pharaoh for his people; then he received the Law and led his people through the wilderness. Moreover, he accepted the advice of Jethro his father-in-law, when he counselled that Moses should share the administrative responsibility of Israel (Exodus 18:18). But meanwhile it must be acknowledged that Jethro had accepted the faith of Israel (Exodus 18:9). Furthermore, in Numbers chapter twelve, the attempt by Aaron and Miriam to rebuke Moses for his marriage to an Ethiopian woman was immediately countered by the Lord's direct intervention and judgment on Miriam, who, as the woman, was probably the most outspoken critic.

Next, we turn to 1 Kings 11:1–8 where we read the story of Solomon's declension. His extraordinary gift of wisdom was not sufficient to prevent him from falling, and leading him into a state of spiritual darkness. The son of the pious David, the religiously trained child of Bathsheba (Proverbs 31:1–3), the pupil of Nathan, instead of showing maturity with experience, became an old and foolish king. And his fall is primarily attributed to his marriages. 'But King Solomon loved many strange women, together with the daughter of Pharaoh, women of the Moabites, Ammonites, Edomites, Zidonians and Hittites; of the nations concerning which the Lord said unto the children of Israel, Ye shall not go in to them, neither shall they come in unto you: for surely they will turn away your heart after their gods . . .' (1 Kings 11:1, 2). His wives did draw him into idolatry and he accommodated pagan gods in Jerusalem, 'And the Lord was angry with Solomon, because his heart was turned from the Lord God of Israel . . .' (1 Kings 11:9). Again an inter-racial marriage is condemned because of the spiritual decline which resulted from it, not because it was contracted between persons of different racial groups. (Polygamy was permitted and practised in those days; in fact it frequently signified position and wealth.) Perhaps it should be pointed out that his marriage to Pharaoh's daughter (of Egypt) is not censured in Scripture (1 Kings 3:1), though it has been questioned whether it was in conformity with the Law (see Exodus 34:16); Psalm 45 and the Song of Songs are said to have been composed in her honour. However, it would seem from Psalm 45:10, 11 that Solomon required that she renounce her idolatry before contracting into marriage—but this he did not do with the 'strange women' in his old age.

Finally, there is the delightfully simple record of Ruth and

Boaz. The record begins with Elimelech and Naomi being driven from their native land of Israel into Moab by famine, where their two sons Mahlon and Chilion (identified by some as Joash and Saraph in 1 Chronicles 4:22) married Moabitish girls, and where Elimelech himself died. The two sons also died, and Naomi decided to make her way back to Israel. Ruth, the widow of the younger son, insisted on accompanying her, 'Whither thou goest I will go, and where thou lodgest I will lodge; thy people shall be my people, and thy God my God'. The story is thus a lesson in loyalty. Ruth, in devotion to Naomi, insists on remaining at her side, and in loyalty to God—for she had embraced the true religion—wanted to maintain true worship. On reaching Bethlehem, she meets Boaz whilst gleaning in his fields, and eventually marries him (Ruth 4:13). This chapter concludes with a brief list of their descendants showing that David was of their line. In other words, through this inter-racial marriage, where both parties were worshippers of the true God, the Lord Jesus himself is descended.

In conclusion, the references to inter-racial marriage in the Old Testament do not forbid marriage on racial grounds at all. The purity of religion is the predominant factor in all the passages we have discussed.

THE PRINCIPLE OF MARRIAGE IN THE NEW TESTAMENT

In the New Testament the one command to believers that is paramount is that marriage to an unbeliever is to be avoided. 'Be ye not unequally yoked together with unbelievers: for what fellowship hath righteousness with unrighteousness? and what communion hath light with darkness?' (2 Cor. 6:14). The reason given for this injunction is interesting (verses 15 and 16), 'Ye are the temple of the living God . . .' This is one of the great revealing phrases of Scripture, conveying a wonderful revelation in a few words. The Spirit of God dwells in the hearts and lives of believers, and God has no fellowship with Satan. Therefore, believers cannot marry unbelievers. This is the principle which is found consistently throughout the New Testament. At the beginning of the mission of the New Testament Church, God revealed to Peter that the Gentiles were to be included. In Acts chapter ten we read of Peter's vision of 'a great sheet, knit at the four corners, and let down to the earth: wherein were all manner of fourfooted beasts of the earth, and wild beasts, and creeping things, and fowls of the air' (Acts 10:11, 12). Peter refused to eat, protesting that the meat was common and unclean. A voice from heaven replied,

'What God hath cleansed, that call not thou common' (verse 15). This was repeated three times—and then the Gentile, Cornelius, sent for Peter desiring to know the true God. Peter went to see him, and instructed him, interpreting his vision as a revelation from God to extend the Church to the Gentiles. Thus the nature of the one universal Church was revealed. No one was common or unclean, because of their ethnic origin. God cleansed believing Jew or believing Gentile in the same way.

The problem text

'And hath determined the times before appointed, and the bounds of their habitation' (Acts 17:26). This is an oft-quoted text used to oppose immigration, desegregation and inter-racial marriage. Isolated from its context it might seem a powerful argument but we need to examine the whole chapter before arriving at a conclusion. Paul is in Athens, the centre of Hellenistic culture and a city 'wholly given to idols'. Petronius, a contemporary writer at Nero's court, says satirically that it was easier to find a god at Athens than a man. This 'stirred the spirit' of the Apostle. And when he saw the multitude of altars to the various gods who were supposed to care for every circumstance in life, including one to the 'unknown god', he realised that his message to the people of Athens necessitated a different approach, though his speech at Lystra has certain similarities.

Paul begins his discourse by 'revealing the unknown God'—who made the world and all therein—and dwelleth in temples not made with hands. He developed his argument by saying that this God, the great Creator, 'giveth to all life, and breath, and all things' (v. 25) and 'hath made of one blood all nations of men for to dwell on all the face of the earth' (v. 26). Thus the Apostle sees the whole human race stemming from one source. He continues, 'and hath determined the times before appointed, and the bounds of their habitation'. In this verse the Apostle is basically opposing the Epicurians' emphasis on CHANCE and the Stoics' doctrine of FATE, ascribing the periods and localities in which men and nations flourish to the sovereign will of the living God. He continues with the argument that all men, therefore, ought to seek the one living God. Thus this verse, interpreted in its context, cannot really be used to justify segregation, or to oppose inter-racial marriage. It has absolutely no bearing on either.

Finally it should be remembered that Timothy was the child of a mixed marriage, his mother being a Jew, and his father a Greek

(Acts 16:1). This fact did not prevent his becoming a tool in the hand of the Lord in any way.

At this point we must examine the nature of the Kingdom of God as revealed in both Testaments. The Old Testament prophets proclaimed the idea of a Theocracy. Their prime message was that God had chosen Israel to be his people (they were elected from the nations) and had established a covenant relationship between them and himself. This involved the keeping of the Law and the unwritten law of love in their hearts. The covenant would establish the Kingdom of God on earth. The Kingdom the prophets saw was an earthly, visible, tangible Kingdom—inhabited by God-fearing, covenant-keeping men and women, who married as well as worshipped. Moreover, prophecy at its highest points went beyond the bounds of the natural Israel. 'For the earth shall be full of the knowledge of the Lord, as the waters cover the sea' (Isaiah 11:9).

'All the ends of the world shall remember and return unto the Lord: and all the kindreds of the nations shall worship before thee. For the kingdom is the Lord's, and he is the governor among the nations' (Psalm 22:27, 28). The Rev. G. Groggan gives an excellent exegesis of the common origin of man in Genesis chapter two and also points out how the expansion of the human race led to the dispersion of peoples after Babel. Although the prophets all sprang from the people of Israel their highest aspirations included the peoples of all the nations. They would not live to see it, but the Kingdom would be extended to all peoples . . . and as pioneers of truth as well as morality they could understand it, proclaim it and work towards it.

The coming of the King is without question a milestone in the history of the Kingdom. The detailed genealogies at the beginning of two of the Gospels, usually 'skipped' by the casual reader, are of uttermost importance. The interesting fact to note is the difference between the two. The genealogy in Matthew 1:1–16 goes back as far as Abraham—the Father of the Jewish nation: the genealogy in Luke 3:23–38 goes back to Adam, the father of mankind. The genealogy in Matthew is that of Joseph, while that in Luke is Mary's. Luke 3:23 says, 'Jesus himself . . . being (as was supposed) the son of Joseph, which was the son of Heli.' The explanation, for those who may see a difficulty in this, is that Joseph was the son-in-law of Heli, who was, like himself a descendant

75

of David. 'Son' is not in the Greek, but is rightly supplied by the translators, and would accord with Jewish usage.

Thus, whether we appeal to Jewish or Gentile law of descent, or matrilineal or patrilineal line of ancestry, both Gospels declare that Jesus Christ was not only the Jewish Messiah, but the Saviour of all peoples. To use the phraseology we have been using in this chapter, he, and he alone, is the inter-racial Saviour. This truth is more clearly seen in the New Testament.

Jesus said, 'I am the way, the truth, and the life: no man cometh unto the Father, but by me' (John 14:6), and 'I am the door of the sheep. All that ever came before me are thieves and robbers: but the sheep did not hear them. I am the door: by me if any man enter in, he shall be saved' (John 10:7–9).

Peter said, 'Neither is there salvation in any other: for there is none other name under heaven given among men, whereby we must be saved' (Acts 4:12). Paul wrote, 'For there is one God, and one mediator between God and men, the man Christ Jesus; *who gave himself a ransom for all*' (1 Timothy 2:5, 6). Basically both Testaments make plain the fundamental truths: the sinfulness of man, the one way of salvation and the brotherhood of the re-deemed in Jesus. There is not, nor can there be, any distinction because of race. The Centurion, the Ethiopian Eunuch, the Philippian jailor . . . and so to the Gentile world and all peoples. The Christian faith is the faith of the 'uttermost parts'. There is but one Church—the Church of the redeemed.

We can now consider the relationship of believers, firstly to God and then to each other. In the model prayer, Jesus taught his followers to pray, 'Our Father . . .' The pronoun 'Our' is all embracing. Paul, in his major theological treatise, says, 'Is he the God of the Jews only? Is he not also of the Gentiles? Yes, of the Gentiles also: seeing it is one God, which shall justify the circumcision by faith, and uncircumcision through faith' (Romans 3:29, 30). And continues, 'For as many as are led by the Spirit of God, they are the sons of God . . . Ye have received the Spirit of adoption, whereby we cry, Abba, Father' (Romans 8:14, 15).

At the moment of conversion, man becomes 'a son of God'. There is never a distinction of race or colour. The Kingdom of God is composed of men of faith, they live, work, witness and worship together. The intimate relationship of marriage provides no exception.

There may not be any definite reason why two people should not be married—but occasionally there are circumstances which may make marriage inadvisable. For example, many would deny that there remains any class distinction in England. Yet when marriage is contemplated the question of class does undeniably count as a factor, particularly with the respective parents. One young couple, known to the writer, were advised by a clergyman not to marry, simply on the grounds of different class; and the engagement was eventually broken off. Although inter-racial marriage cannot be said to be against scriptural teaching, yet the Church has a responsibility to ensure that those being married are aware of the sanctity of marriage and of the solemnity of the marriage vows and there may be circumstances in which marriage is inadvisable. This, of course, applies to any marriage, and not only to inter-racial ones. Before the marriage ceremony the following words are often used,

> 'Marriage is an honourable estate to all who enter it lawfully and in true affection. It was hallowed by our Lord's most solemn words, and adorned by his presence at the marriage feast in Cana of Galilee; it is a means of grace to all who are called to it of God and rightly use it. And it has been consecrated by the faithful bond of good men and good women in every generation; therefore it ought to be entered upon reverently, discreetly, advisedly, and in the fear of God.'

This exhortation is based on the spirit of Scripture and few would deny that other factors should be taken into account. It is the purpose of this section to examine those factors, in relation to inter-racial marriage.

The last two decades have seen a considerable increase in our understanding of other cultures—and the study of sociology is still increasing. With it comes a deepening respect for other ways of life and social structures. Culture must be taken into account.

Before writing this paragraph a considerable number of letters were written to church and mission leaders asking their views. The vast majority gave a word of warning regarding the continuing real happiness of the couple. One for instance, said, 'The cultures are still so disparate that difficulties are bound to arise . . .'. With this warning we must progress in our study, with only the passing comment that if a couple from different cultures do marry they must both be prepared to make adjustments to their traditional ways. On the other hand, several couples who had married across race denied any real difficulties, other than the adjustment experienced by nearly all young couples in early married life. The problems, said two couples at a joint meeting with the writer, are with the onlookers—not with the couples themselves. 'Everyone expects us to have difficulties but there are none.'

As to the social acceptance of couples married across supposed cultural borders, the main factor is the place of residence. Predominant local thought is important for it is virtually impossible to live dissociated from society. An African married to an English person living in the United Kingdom would tend to live as the English do. The main responsibility for adjustment would be with the African. Similarly an Englishman marrying an African and living in Africa may find difficulties.

On the other hand, some areas do not appear to have a racial or colour problem. In Brazil, for example, there would be no difficulty, for the ninety millions of people are of all shades from black to white, and marriage between people of differing colour shades and with foreigners presents no problems. Again in the cosmopolitan and tolerant society of Singapore there is no difficulty. One pastor likened his congregation to a 'kind of United Nations'.

This leads us to consider the social acceptance of couples married across race (different social origins and physical features) as distinct from across culture (different customs, language, thought patterns and family structure). One such couple, the husband originating from Guyana, and the wife from Australia, were both raised in British culture, yet both expressed the same fears when contemplating marriage. The husband said in an interview, 'I was scared what other Christians might think.' The wife had similar fears. She said, 'The thing that really made us sure was that we prayed about it so much and we even laid "fleeces" because of the implications of a "mixed marriage". The Lord answered these "fleeces" in a very real and almost frightening way.' The couple were accepted by their local church, in London, and said that they did not suffer to any extent in the community outside, apart from an occasional jibe. For example the wife was once called 'a dirty white cow'; and when travelling together, carrying a guitar, they were called 'the black and white minstrels'. The couple expressed their experience thus—'we have no problems about our marriage; the problems are largely in other peoples' minds—and they are their problems.'

78

CHILDREN

'Are you going to have children?'

'Children? I don't know what you would call a marriage without children, but it certainly wouldn't be marriage,' replied Sidney Poitier in the sound track of *Guess Who's Coming to Dinner?*, the controversial film on race relations. The film debates many issues involved in inter-racial marriages, and depicts clearly the changing attitudes of all involved. Initially both sets of parents were shocked. This gradually subsided into surprise and then to acceptance of the inevitable. The coloured maid in the girl's household railed on Poitier accusing him of betraying their race. For two hours the families talked, and talked, weighing up the pros and cons—but it seemed that the wedding went forward, and the children were to be a natural sequence.

As to the Christian position, some experienced Christian leaders consider that the children of these marriages face severe problems. Others equally experienced disagree fundamentally. In any case, it was felt that it was for the couples involved to make a final decision for themselves. The truth is that these children expose the racial prejudices in other people's minds, and therein lies the problem.

Finally, we must look into history, for experience is a good teacher. The racial problems of Africa started with the 'discovery' of the continent and its subsequent colonisation by developed European powers. The slave trade period, with its dehumanisation of the black man, can never be forgotten by Africans. The recent anti-west moves—such as the removal of whites from administrative positions, restricted visas for whites, etc. are provoked by memories of the past. Although slavery is at the basis of black experience of white colonialism, the slave trade was eventually abolished, but 'progress' from that point onwards left an equally notorious mark. Even missionary books often give the impression that African culture is essentially bad and European good. The general thought pattern nurtured during the colonial period was 'black bad, white good' and with that a definite racist problem grew. Moreover, because whites were in the superior position, educationally, economically and simply because they played the role of conquerors the white superiority complex grew. The white was always the teacher, administrator, governor, and therefore better than the black. This mentality hardened, until the truth of the fundamental equality of man as propounded in the Scriptures became obscured. Now the pendulum has swung, resulting in a violent black reaction and both black and white need to look again at their Bibles. A few have rediscovered the truth: marriage is the result, the critics being those with the traditional superiority complex.

In America there has been a colour problem ever since slaves were introduced in large numbers in the eighteenth century. In early years they were subjected to the indignities of being herded like cattle and bought and sold in markets, and were subject to chattel law. Laws were passed forbidding marriage. Many whites saw the injustice of the situation, and an abolitionist group developed, which eventually thrust the entire land into civil war. Legislation slowly improved the status of the Negro, and by 1866 he was guaranteed citizenship rights and allowed to hold office. By 1957 public gardens, parks, libraries and professional organisations were desegregated. It was not until 1967 that the US Supreme Court ruled that laws in various States forbidding Negro/white marriages were unconstitutional. However, inter-racial marriages have been increasing for several years, and even if this ruling had not swept away remaining anti-miscegenation statutes, it is doubtful if any legislation could have controlled it. The battle in the USA has been a long and bitter one, lasting about 100 years. Now the Supreme Court has reached the logical conclusion that because men are equal irrespective of colour or ethnic origin, it is illogical to forbid inter-racial marriage.

Perhaps brief mention should be made of the situation in South Africa. South Africa is attempting to turn back the wheels of history to a pre-colonial situation. The black tribes, which have always tended to be nomadic, are being ushered into 'reserves' which theoretically are self-governing, and where tribal laws and customs may be perpetuated. Whites congregate in the towns, where the only blacks allowed belong to the servant categories. There is a definite line of demarcation drawn, and enforced, in every walk of life. Thus marriage between the groups is strictly forbidden, simply because it would cross the line. Even intercourse between white and black is punishable by imprisonment or a fine.

CONCLUSIONS

The witnessing Christian of the twentieth century has a new responsibility to meet the problems surrounding race relations. First of all, let him take his Bible and study the Scriptures once again. Let him underline those passages dealing with the common origin of man, and the unity of the Church. Any who have a part in the white supremacy system must radically change and any who are liberal minded paternalists retaining a 'let's help the poor black folk' attitude remember that it is not the teaching of Scripture. But integration is a two-way process, and those born coloured should dismiss their inferiority complex, take their rightful place in the community, avoiding excesses which in the end only accentuate racial problems. Integration demands action more than spiritual understanding and sympathy. The Christian's task irrespective of the colour of his skin, is to proclaim to the world the equality of man, but let him not start until he is willing to give his son or daughter in marriage to a believer of another race.

Bridge Over Troubled Waters

LEIGHTON FORD

On a warm spring Sunday I was the guest preacher in a very beautiful and fashionable church that had impeccable credentials for its orthodox Christianity. The sanctuary was packed. The music was outstanding. The atmosphere was reverent. The people were eager and attentive. I spoke that morning about Jesus' encounter with a social outcast, a scoundrel of a tax collector named Zacchaeus, an encounter that illustrated Jesus' longing to 'seek and save those who are lost'. Afterwards the comments were warm and gratifying.

Later that day, to my dismay, I heard that some Negro people had tried to enter the church for the service and had been refused admission by the ushers. Some weeks before, the church had been the target of a racial demonstration. As a result the church officials had decided, as a matter of policy, that Negroes arriving at the church in groups of two or more would automatically be assumed to be demonstrators, not worshippers, and would be denied entrance. And apparently the several Negroes who came that morning had arrived together rather than singly, and the policy had been applied to them.

Some further reports produced the information that one of the black visitors had been a soldier from a nearby military base, due to leave in a few days for Vietnam. Having read in the paper that a Billy Graham Team member would preach at that church on Sunday morning, and knowing of Billy Graham's reputation for preaching to all people, he had set out to find the church, but found the door barred to him.

Anguish would hardly be strong enough to describe what I felt. Here I was preaching about a Christ who came in love and openness to society's outcasts, and the church that represented that Christ was barred to a black man, who as it turned out, might well confront death shortly. What the man's motives in coming were I do not fully know. Some people later suggested that he had been 'prompted' to come by some out-of-state agitators. But whatever

82

his motives I could not help but think that Zacchaeus' motives were fairly murky. Apparently sheer curiosity led him down to see Jesus passing through Jericho. Nevertheless Jesus welcomed him and went to stay at his home.

We located the name and address of that soldier and I wrote to him, expressing my personal apology, and assuring him of a welcome to any future service in which I might be taking part. I wrote to the pastor of the church (who no doubt found himself pulled from one side by reactionaries and attacked from the other by radicals) and expressed to him my own protest at the policy they had established. I issued a public statement that I would never knowingly speak in a church that had racial bars. And later when a clergyman friend of mine was going to Vietnam I arranged for him to contact the soldier, give him my personal greetings, and witness to him of the love of Christ.

Yet when all this was done, there remained the sobering sense that we Christians have so far to go in obeying the implications of the Gospel of Christ in terms of our love for all men.

If you read the New Testament, you can't help but see how Jesus broke down all the barriers that might have divided man from man. When he chose Simon the Zealot as a disciple he broke down political barriers. By dining with Zacchaeus he ignored class barriers. In talking with a woman of Samaria he put aside social barriers. In heeding the appeal of the Syrophoenician woman and praising the faith of the Roman centurion, he bypassed racial and national barriers. He allowed a woman who was a sinner to touch him, quietly forgetting the barrier of reputation. A poor widow gave her mite and he held her up for praise, overlooking economic barriers. When the disciples' feet were dirty he washed them, not minding the barrier between master and servant. Yet when the disciples criticised a follower who did not belong to their group he rebuked their intolerance, setting aside denominational barriers. As a baby, an old man rejoiced in him; as a young man, children flocked to him; he crossed the gaps of age. He was a bridge across troubled waters. His love never was stopped by a wall.

When the Christian revolution first began, Jesus Christ not only brought man into a new relationship with God. He also broke down the walls between men. He brought about a social revolution. As Mary put it in the Magnificat, 'He has put down the mighty from their thrones, and exalted those of low degree' (Lk. 1:52 RSV).

In the city of Antioch we see this social revolution at work. 'In the church at Antioch there were prophets and teachers, Barnabas, Symeon, who was called Niger, Lucius of Cyrene, Manaen a member of the court of Herod the tetrarch, and Saul' (Acts 13:1 RSV). There were two Jews, two Africans and a Roman aristocrat. All races and classes had become beautiful in Christ.

In sad contrast, it is to the shame of the Christian Church that we have been so slow to face the demands of the gospel in the twentieth-century racial revolution. With some notable exceptions we have moved only when we have been run over from behind. Too many white Christians have supposed they enjoy a privileged position at some 'white hand of God'.

What does this have to do with the gospel? Well, let me ask what kind of gospel we are preaching when a church sends missionaries to convert Africans but suggests to the black man at home that he go to his own church with his own kind? Why should the Negro listen to us talking about a home in Heaven when we refuse to make him at home in our neighbourhood and our school? I cannot forget the burden of a friend of mine, ministering in a certain town where age-old prejudices have held fast. He said, 'I want to do something to help win Negroes in our town to Christ, but it seems like such a mockery to try to evangelise them when I can't even invite them to come and worship in my church'. What, I ask you, does this have to do with the gospel and evangelism?

Our world has been torn apart by racial crises. Lord Carradon, when he was United Kingdom Ambassador to the United Nations, said, 'I am convinced that race is the most explosive and dangerous issue the world must face.' What does the Bible have to say in this crisis?

It is basic to the teachings of the Bible that mankind as God's creation is one, biologically and spiritually. The first chapters of Genesis show all men coming from a single pair. After the flood destroyed the ancient world, unity was restored to man through Noah's family. Paul took this idea of man's biological unity to affirm that man also has a spiritual affinity that made it possible for sin to spread to all men. 'As sin came into the world through one man and death through sin, so death spread to all men because all men sinned' (Romans 5:12 RSV). When Paul talked to the philosophers on Mars Hill in Athens, he stressed that God 'made from one every nation of men to live on all the face of earth' (Acts 17:26 RSV).

84

Another clear teaching of the Bible is that all men have a special importance and dignity because they have been created in the image of God (Genesis 1:26–7). Regardless of a man's race or class or background he is stamped with this image. So James 3:9 warns us not to 'curse men who are made in the likeness of God' (RSV)

In a fascinating interview on British television, Prince Philip commented on a widespread range of subjects. When he was asked about racism the Prince pointed out that race is not simply a matter of colour. 'What is distinctive of the Scot or the Welshman but race?' he asked. 'There is a lot of tribalism in us still.' He went on to point out that a few hundred years ago there was only one book that everybody in the western world read—the Bible. Today, however, we get our intellectual and moral nourishment from a thousand sources, radio, television, books and newspapers. 'In the days of God, so to speak,' Prince Philip noted, 'everyone was seen as equal in the sight of God. This made for anti-racism. But take away God and we have to revert to tribalism again.'

Not only does the Bible tell us that men were made by God and in God's image, but that all men also stand guilty before God. This is a common teaching in both the Old Testament and the New Testament. Isaiah confessed, 'All we like sheep have gone astray; we have turned every one to his own way' (Isaiah 53:6 RSV), while Paul plainly indicted the whole human race, Jew and pagan alike, 'For all have sinned, and come short of the glory of God' (Romans 3:23 AV). A spiritual disease infects every race of men.

One glaring result of man's spiritual rebellion against God is racism. This rebellion is dramatised in Genesis 11, where we find the story of the Tower of Babel. Men decided to build a city with its top in the heavens to express their spiritual arrogance. When the Lord saw the pride of man he confused their languages so that they could not understand one another's speech, and he scattered them over the face of the earth. This act of God at Babel was a punishment for man's pride. It was also a preventive measure to protect man from destroying himself with some kind of absolute sinful power.

There are many people who believe that the Bible teaches that black men are especially cursed by God. For example, I have heard people say that Negroes are descended from Ham, one of Noah's sons, and that God condemned them to be slaves forever. A careful reading of Genesis 9 explodes this theory. Noah fell into a drunken stupor one day and one of his sons Ham, saw his father as he lay naked in his tent. Ham told his two brothers outside. The other brothers took a garment, and walked backwards and covered the nakedness of their father; they turned their faces away so they would not see their father's nakedness. When Noah awoke he realised how Ham had shamed him. He pronounced a curse upon one of Ham's sons, Canaan, and said that he would be a slave to his brothers. Racists around the world have twisted this passage to fit their own prejudices, saying that the black man is descended from Canaan. Actually, however, it was Cush, another son of Ham, not Canaan, from whom the Ethiopians, the Africans, descended. So the theory of the black man's curse is a flimsy falsehood, completely without foundation.

It is worth noting that the Old Testament as well as the New condemns racism. Numbers 12 relates that when Moses married a Cushite woman, an Ethiopian, his brother and sister, Aaron and Miriam, despised and spoke against Moses. Apparently they despised this inter-racial marriage. In answer, God judged Aaron and Miriam for their prejudice and caused leprosy to come upon them.

Certainly God gives different gifts and different privileges to different people. The Bible does not flatten all men out in a kind of bland equality. As Jesus taught, some men may have one talent, some two, some may have five or ten. Yet the Scripture teaches over and over that 'God is not a respecter of persons'. That principle is repeated at least eight different times in the Bible. It applies to man's acceptance with God. Peter said 'Truly I perceive that God shows no partiality, but in every nation anyone who fears him and does what is right is acceptable to him' (Acts 10:34–5 RSV). It should determine the nature of relationships between Christian masters and slaves, employers and employees. Paul taught, 'Masters . . . forbear threatening, knowing that he who is both their Master and yours is in heaven and that there is no partiality with him' (Ephesians 6:9 RSV). It applies to the judgment of God 'for the wrongdoer will be paid back for the wrong he has done and there is no partiality' (Colossians 3:25 RSV). This principle guides the treatment of the poor in the Christian Church. 'My brethren, show no partiality as you hold the faith of our Lord Jesus Christ, the Lord of Glory' (James 2:1 RSV).

The Scripture also tells us that there is one Saviour for all men Jesus Christ, and that the way of salvation is open to all, 'for there is no distinction between Jew and Greek; the same Lord is Lord of all and bestows his riches upon all who call upon him. For "every one who calls upon the name of the Lord will be saved"' (Romans 10:12–13 RSV). In the time of Jesus there was no greater division than that between Jew and Gentile. Yet Paul could say that Christ reconciled both 'to God in one body through the cross, there by bringing the hostility to an end' (Ephesians 2:16 RSV). God transcended the differences by giving to Jew and Gentile a new status. All blood-bought believers were brothers in Christ.

In our Crusades around the world we have seen black and white, young and old, the rich with their minks and the poor with their shabby clothes coming forward to trust the same Saviour. The ground is surely level at the foot of the cross! At a time of grave crisis in Alabama President Lyndon Johnson requested Billy Graham to hold meetings across the length and breadth of the state. Cancelling other plans, Dr. Graham did so. Inter-racial meetings, some of them the first in history, were held in cities large and small. I remember sitting in the Crampton Bowl in Montgomery. Half the crowd was black and half was white. There together singing the same hymns, saying the same prayers to the same God, there was a unity. One aristocratic white lady came forward at the invitation to stand by the platform. A Negro lady came and counselled her. Afterwards someone asked the white lady if she minded a Negro counselling her. Her reply: 'Did a Negro counsel me?' She had become oblivious to the difference of race in the light of Christ.

The Bible also teaches that there is one Holy Spirit who baptises all who have been born again into the one body of Christ, the Church (1 Corinthians 12:13). As a devout Jewish boy, Paul had been taught to thank God that he had not been born a Gentile, a slave, or a woman. But when he became a free man in Christ he wrote to the Galatians, 'There is neither Jew nor Greek, there is neither slave nor free, there is neither male nor female, for you are all one in Christ Jesus' (Galatians 3:28 RSV). Racial superiority was gone: 'there is neither Jew nor Greek'. Every race, colour and language was included in the offer of salvation through faith in Christ. Class superiority was gone: 'there is neither slave nor free'. Pride of face or grace or race had disappeared in a common loyalty to Jesus! Sexual superiority was gone: 'there is neither male nor female'. Feminists should take note: Paul, whom many supposed to have been anti-female, asserted that in Christ male and female were one and equal, and he did this in a world in which women were despised and often exploited.

Of course, all this doesn't mean that racial, social, and sexual differences are literally gone. After one becomes a Christian he is still black or white, illiterate or highly educated, man or woman. When we say that Christ has nullified these distinctions, we do not mean that they are not there. We mean that they do not matter. They still exist but no longer do they create any barriers to fellowship.

Racism was a widespread problem in the ancient world. For example, the Fourth Gospel tells us that 'the Jews have no dealings with the Samaritans' (John 4:9 AV). A wall of bitterness and hatred stood between the two races. The shortest route for Jews to take from Galilee to Judea was through Samaria, but they habitually took a roundabout route to avoid facing their enemies. When the Jews wanted to insult Jesus they said he was a Samaritan and had a demon. Jesus refused to go along with this racial prejudice. He deliberately went to Samaria on different occasions. When he healed ten lepers he reminded men that the only one who returned to say thanks was a Samaritan. It was a Samaritan who was the hero of his parable of the man who fell among thieves. In broad daylight he talked with a Samaritan woman of bad reputation by the well of Sychar (John 4:7ff). His evangelistic orders to his disciples included Samaria in their itinerary (Acts 1:8).

It was not easy for the early Christians to follow Jesus' teachings and practice wholeheartedly. There was a struggle before Samaritans and other Gentiles were admitted into full fellowship. A top-level investigating committee had to be sent to make sure the Samaritan believers were genuine Christians (Acts 8:14).

All this should be a lesson to us that prejudice does not automatically leave at conversion. Long after Peter began to follow Jesus, God had an assignment for him to go tell the good news to a God-fearing Roman Army officer named Cornelius. Knowing that Peter, as a Jew, would rebel against contact with a Gentile, he first sent Peter a vision of a great sheet let down from Heaven with all kinds of animals and birds and told him to eat. Peter refused to eat what he as a Jew had been taught was 'unclean food' until God said, 'Peter, what God says is kosher you must not call common.' Peter had to learn that God was cleansing and accepting Gentiles as well as Jews, that God 'shows no partiality' but accepts those 'in every nation who fear him' (Acts 10:35).

Many Christians have yet to let Christ revolutionise racial attitudes. Like Peter we need to have the Holy Spirit change this area of our lives. Paul Rees tells of meeting an American sergeant in Japan who had been trying to witness to another sergeant, a black man, about Christ. Three times the other man was nearly ready to accept Christ but each time he stopped short. At last the Negro sergeant disclosed what was holding him back. Painfully, he uncovered his real hesitation. 'Look', he said, 'if I accept Christ I can go to chapel with you here in Japan. Right? But can I go to church with you when we get back home?' The Christian sergeant was stopped short. He knew that his friend would not be welcome back home and he said, 'Dr. Rees, God had to bring me all the way to Japan to see that there is a relation between Jesus Christ and this race thing.'

What can I do? People all over America and the world are asking that question as we face the pent-up boiling forces of racial turbulence.

We can rejoice and be glad that God has made a colourful world. There are eighty-eight keys on the piano. Play only the white keys, you get some music. Play only the black keys, you get other music. But you have to play both black and white to have harmony and great music. So God has a plan for all the races. The black man doesn't need to be made in the image of the white man or the white man in the image of the black. We all need to learn by the grace of God to reflect his Image!

Equally important is the frank facing of racism in our own hearts. Few people will admit to being outright bigots any more. We like to protest, 'I don't have any prejudice!' But inside, each of us does have areas of deliberate misunderstanding. Sin affects each of us, cuts us off from God, makes us insecure; so we try to gain a feeling of security by cutting someone else down, perhaps someone of another race. This is a subtle process that infects each of us. The first step in really coming to know the power of Jesus Christ is a genuine honesty, an honesty that is willing to let God search our hearts and show us in our own lives areas where we need cleansing.

We must learn to accept freely the fact that God accepts us as we are when we come to him in faith and let the 'blood of Jesus Christ, God's Son, cleanse us from all sin'. God can wipe away the stain of prejudice. A lot of so-called race relations have been built on guilt, fear, and manipulation by both sides. This is a poor basis for understanding. Guilt covers over what is inside us and festers into fear and resentment that poisons. Grace, on the other hand, opens us up and produces genuine love.

And further, we can let God show each of us a place where we can build a bridge. This is not a matter of running helter-skelter in a hundred different directions. It is a matter of quietly letting the Holy Spirit direct each one of us to do what lies within our power. This will mean sharing the Christ who can change men's hearts. It will mean supporting laws that oppose all kinds of discriminations. Laws can not make people love one another but they can help to prevent flagrant injustice. We can make friends with those of other races. Church leaders can arrange programmes of exchange visits with people from churches of other races and make sure that their own churches are known to be open to all races in Christ's name. Businessmen and Union officials can help open up places for individuals from minority groups. If we want to act, there is something for each of us to do!

Housing is a most crucial area in which Christians may exert their influence. Many blacks feel that the key to the solution of other racial problems—such as school integration—lies in the availability of good housing to those who can afford it regardless of race. However, the phrase 'open housing' arouses emotion and fear in some people more than almost any other aspect of the race situation. The unscrupulous salesman will prey on such fears to conjure up visions of black invasions and plummeting property values. In such a situation, what will the Christian do? Will he too panic and run? Will he sound off as a self-righteous saint who has all the answers and none of the concerns of his neighbours? Or will he be able to pose a constructive alternative?

Often Christians acting together can do more than they can as individuals. One of my colleagues, Howard Jones, tells two stories illustrating how two churches exerted their influence on housing in diametrically opposite directions. In the first instance, a friend took him to see a beautiful large church plant in a major city. Once, these buildings had been owned by a large white congregation with an outstanding record for support of world missions. Now on the steeple was painted a Muslim crescent. When the first Negro (a well-to-do professional man) moved into that neighbourhood, the church panicked and put their property up for sale. But they were unable to find a church group to buy it and finally sold it to a real-estate agent who in turn sold it to the Black Muslims! The congregation moved out to the faraway suburbs and built another expensive plant. Ironically, a week after the dedication of the new sanctuary the first black family moved into their new neighbourhood, which raises the interesting question as to how long they will be able to cut and run!

In complete contrast is another congregation, largely white, just as evangelical as the first church, in a similar neighbourhood but with a vision, faith and courage that is entirely different. The minister of this church invited Howard Jones to come for a Sunday evening presentation on the racial situation from a Scriptural standpoint. After discussion and prayer the people of this church decided to tackle the problem before it arose. They appointed representatives who went to the real-estate firms of the area, told them of their intention to stay and minister where the church was, and courteously requested their co-operation in avoiding any 'flight mentality' or scare-mongering. What the future holds for these people who can predict? Social change and pressure may be so rapid that regardless of what they do the racial make-up of their church and neighbourhood will have to alter. Yet which church will be judged as most faithful to its Lord? Two buildings answer that question: one vacated by Christ's followers who found the price of staying too high, crowned now with Mohammad's symbol; the other where the Cross is still held high.

Jesus Christ is working a quiet revolution in racial affairs. Newark, New Jersey, was called the most dangerous city in America after the recent riots. But in Newark lives Bill Iverson, a man who was burdened to reach youth in the ghettos with the love of Christ. As a first step he bought a lunch counter across from one of the biggest inner-city high schools. Over many months he reached out in friendship to the young people who came in, winning their trust. His witness across the counter resulted in many of them finding Christ. In the aftermath of his spiritual work, street academies were founded for school dropouts. When Newark was blazing in the terrible riots of 1967, the one shop in that block that was not burned out with a Molotov cocktail was that lunch counter. In the middle of the riots both National Guardsmen and black ghetto residents sat drinking coffee! God had used him as a bridge across troubled waters.

On 4th April 1968, Martin Luther King, Jr., was cut down by a sniper's bullet on a motel balcony in Memphis. In the aftermath of this assassination a huge wave of vengeance battered the United States. On the other side of the continent that wave engulfed and killed another Martin, a white bus driver named Martin Whitted. At the end of his run in a lonely section of Hunters Point in San Francisco, eleven black youths pulled him from his bus, savagely battered him, and left him mortally wounded. Tension and counter-tension rose in the black and white communities. Ugly rumours of violence began to circulate. Fear that the two murders would mean yet more violent outbursts settled on a large part of the community. Then Dixie Whitted, Martin's widow, asked to appear on television. Quietly she spoke of her love for her husband and of her faith in Christ. She told the people she knew how many of them felt but she pleaded with them to refrain from any violence and to be peace-makers instead. Through the power of Jesus Christ, she said, she had no bitterness or hate. She knew that many who were watching wanted not retaliation but reconciliation. Her little community needed recreational facilities for all the young people, and if they wanted to do something, those who were watching could send gifts to build this facility as a memorial to her husband.

The effect was electric! Cynical television crewmen cried and a Stanford co-ed called in to say that her whole life and attitude had been changed by this Christian witness. At the funeral in St. Mark's Lutheran Church, Pastor Ross Hidy said, 'When I married Dixie and Martin six years ago there were two Negroes, friends of theirs, at the wedding'. And when he had finished, three blacks and three whites picked up the coffin and carried it out.

The time has come for a new slogan. We have heard about law power, learning power, earning power. These have their places. So does black power when it means that the black man must forge a place for himself and learn to have a justifiable pride in his own history and race.

But we need another rallying cry today, 'Christ power!' That is the power that can make us love each other. That is the power that can help the white man to turn away from hatred or bigotry or fear. That is the power that can guide the black man or the brown man or the red man away from resentment to use his power with grace and wisdom.

'Christ power!' For the authentic Christ offers us the one way to turn from our hatred, bigotry, and fear; the one way genuinely to build a community of love; the one way to let God flesh out his power in our redeemed humanity, be it black, white, or brown.

Acknowledgments

I am deeply indebted to my wife, Rosemary, for all she did to make this publication possible. Also, I would like to thank Myrtle Powley of Marshall, Morgan and Scott for her work on the manuscript.

Evangelical Responsibility and Racial Tension' was first published in *Spectrum*, and is reprinted by permission.

'The Psychodynamics of Racism' first appeared in *Christianity Today* as two articles under the titles 'The Psychopathology of Racism' and 'The Psychodynamics of Racism' and is reprinted by permission.

'Bridge Over Troubled Waters' is taken from the book *One Way to Change the World* by Leighton Ford, copyright © Harper & Row Publishers Inc. and published in Britain by Coverdale House Publishers.

The lines of poetry on page 21 are from the *Collected Poems* of Alfred Noyes and are quoted by permission of John Murray (Publishers) Ltd.

Index

Biblical References